Back In The
Day At A Place
Called
Galloway

Back In The Day At A Place Called Galloway

Jim Evans

iUniverse

BACK IN THE DAY AT A PLACE CALLED GALLOWAY

iUniverse books may be ordered through booksellers or by contacting:

iUniverse
1663 Liberty Drive
Bloomington, IN 47403
www.iuniverse.com
844-349-9409

Because of the dynamic nature of the Internet, any web addresses or links contained in this book may have changed since publication and may no longer be valid. The views expressed in this work are solely those of the author and do not necessarily reflect the views of the publisher, and the publisher hereby disclaims any responsibility for them.

Any people depicted in stock imagery provided by Getty Images are models, and such images are being used for illustrative purposes only.
Certain stock imagery © Getty Images.

ISBN: 978-1-6632-0201-7 (sc)
ISBN: 978-1-6632-0202-4 (e)

Library of Congress Control Number: 2020914767

Print information available on the last page.

iUniverse rev. date: 09/11/2020

Contents

Dedication

This book is dedicated to my children
Brenda Ruth (Evans) Browy
and
Kenton James Evans

-----The last in the Rogers-Evans lineage to experience
many features of the Galloway described here

Acknowledgments

The author acknowledges the special assistance provided by Dominic ("Dom") Spezialy in preparation of this book. Dom was born and raised in Venango County, Pennsylvania. He lived at Galloway from 1938 until leaving for college following graduation from Rocky Grove High School in 1950. After graduation from Penn State University and serving five years as a navigator in the Air Force, he and his wife, Millie, moved to Alaska where he taught high school classes for seven years. He and his family then returned to the Galloway area for a year where he taught at a local high school before going back to Alaska and resuming teaching for another eighteen years. After retirement, he and Millie served with the Peace Corps in Africa for a two-year period.

Dom has continued to have keen interest in the region of his birth, and during one of his trips "home" spent considerable time at the Venango County Historical Society offices researching the early history of Galloway. In 2015 he contacted me, and we shared memories and information. We considered that organizing it into book-like form might be enjoyable, as well as be of some interest to former and present residents of the region. During the following months Dom sent relevant materials to me, and I began searching through family pictures and memorabilia for the same. But, with many other activities intervening, months turned into years. Although I proceeded in a "fits and starts" manner, the project languished and nearly died. In recent months I picked up the pace, and Dom, along with others mentioned below, proof-read drafts of the manuscript, making suggestions for modifications.

Additionally, I wish to acknowledge assistance of Judy (Jacoby) Lusher, and Grace (Jacoby) Solle, fellow Galloway residents during much of the period of time covered in this book. They proof-read a pre-publication manuscript, gave some suggestions for modifications, and offered some pictures which could be included.

Thank you Dom, Judy and Grace for your help in preparing these stories about years we once shared in that tiny little corner of the world: Galloway, Pennsylvania.

And, thank you, Martha, my wife, for tolerating the many hours I was mentally "absent" from our relationship as I focused on completing this work, including during our present eight week (and counting) home quarantine as we attempt to evade the COVID -19 virus).

Jim Evans
May, 2020
Moore, S.C.

Chapter 1

Introduction

Yes, there really is a place called Galloway, Pennsylvania. You can find it at latitude 41.425, longitude 79.817, altitude 1440 feet; population "maybe 300 to 500", depending on what one considers its boundaries. Or, if you can find an old paper map, it is shown as being in Sugarcreek Township of Venango County on Pennsylvania Route 417 about two miles north of Franklin. Drive up the hill out of Franklin, pass through the village of Rocky Grove and continue for a mile or so until breaking over the top of the hill. There on the right you encounter the sign "Village of Galloway"; and for the next one half to three quarter mile or so you are in the Galloway of this book. In many ways it is the proverbial "wide spot in the road"; not even a traffic light, post office or store. But, it is a place with an interesting history, as well as many memories for the author, and others who have lived there. So, why a book about this tiny piece of real estate unlikely to be of interest to anyone other than a few present or former residents or some of their descendants? There is no single answer. Consider it part autobiography of the author, part a treat for septuagenarians, octogenarians, and beyond who enjoy reminiscing about the "good old days", part a tiny piece of Pennsylvania history, and part a sociological perspective on simpler times in America.

The information presented in the book is from various sources. First and foremost it is from the author's memory bank which hopefully remains as accessible and valid as memory banks can be. That includes especially memories of personal experiences and tales told to me by my mother, Ruth Victoria (Rogers) Evans, who was born, raised and lived most of her eighty-four years at Galloway. As a teenager, I had an unusual for my age interest in history, so also often listened intently to Galloway stories told by my maternal uncle, Robert Wilbur Rogers, and those of a then-octogenarian neighbor, Willis J. Frankenberger, about life during the late 1800s and early 1900s. Entries in the diary of my older sister Margie from the 1930s and 1940s also provide some information. Other information was provided in correspondence with Dominic (Dom) Spezialy, a long-time friend and former Galloway resident with similar interests in its history. Finally, much information came from reference books such as Venango County, Pennsylvania, Her Pioneers and People, by Charles Babcock, an 1866 book titled "Petroleum" by Reverend S. J. M. Eaton, and copies of the Franklin, Pennsylvania newspaper, The News Herald, available on- line through a subscription to Newspapers.com.

Chapter 2

Pre-1859

There is evidence that Galloway and nearby regions were at the lower edges of glaciers as they pushed south during "ice ages". As they proceeded they gouged the earth beneath them, carving out large craters, and pushing masses of rocks ahead of them. This gave rise to basic features of the present landscape. As the earth eventually warmed and glaciers receded, some craters became lakes, such as nearby Conneaut Lake and Sugar Lake. Some rock masses, known as terminal moraines, remained. Of special relevance here is that one such rocky region is on the hillside below the author's childhood Galloway home. It extended at least a half mile down from there, inspiring artist, teacher and Galloway resident Jennie (Braden) Harper to name the school where she taught "Rocky Grove". That name later was adopted by the surrounding community.

Fast forward a few millennia from the last ice age, and there are some written records of what life was like in Venango County during the 18th, and early 19th centuries. According to Eaton (1866), during the 18th century the main human inhabitants of the region were native Americans, mainly of the

Iroquois Tribe. They often interacted with local settlers from Europe who engaged primarily in farming, and fur trading. During the middle part of that century there was great rivalry between France and England for control of various portions of North America, including northwestern Pennsylvania. The French and Indian War occurred during that era (1754 to 1763). These also were the times when France had a fort on the Allegheny River at Franklin, followed later by English forts in the same general location. And, it was during those times that General George Washington was dispatched to the region to mediate settlements with the French over control of the lands. He passed through Franklin on his travel from Pittsburgh to Fort LeBeuf south of Erie. There are reports that his route included the Patchel Run valley which is an area where many Galloway residents later lived, and/or worked in the oil fields.

As noted, farming was a main occupation of those who had immigrated to the region. The History of Venango County text provides some insight into their daily lives during the 18th century. As readily can be imagined, their life was difficult. There were long hours of hard work, a high incidence of infant mortality due to epidemics of disease such as cholera, and little time for socializing. A main concern for many was protecting their sheep herds and cattle from predators such as panthers and wolves. Due in part to necessity, there was much mutual cooperation. Although social activities often centered around church, the Venango County history reference includes mention of enjoyable get-togethers of multiple neighbors to share the meat after a bear or deer had been killed.

In addition to farming, by the middle of the 19th century many persons in the county worked in the iron making, and logging industries. It was stated in the Eaton reference that at one point during the 1840s there were at least seventeen iron furnaces in Venango County. Remains of one near Wyattville still could be seen as late as the 1950s, and perhaps longer. Many parts of the county were rich in a high grade iron ore. There were plenty of trees to use in preparing the charcoal used as fuel in the furnaces, and ample fast flowing streams to provide water power. A tariff on imported iron had given financial advantage to county iron makers, but by the late 1840s conditions of the tariff changed such that the iron making business no longer was profitable. It soon vanished from the county. By the 1850s most of the prime timber in the county had been cut, and shipped down the Allegheny River to markets, leaving farming as the main occupation in the county. Then on June 5th, 1859 a severe late spring frost struck which decimated crops. Fears of famine occurred, and many settlers were making plans to relocate. However, in August of that year Colonel Drake drilled the first oil well near Titusville, and drastic change came to the county.

Residents of Venango and other counties of northwestern Pennsylvania had no idea of the extent of change to come. They could not have imagined that the black liquid some had observed puddling above ground in places would revolutionize their lives, the lives of their descendants, and lives of persons around the world for the next 160 years and beyond.

As is true for many present and past Galloway residents, my ancestry includes some of those 19th century immigrants to Venango County. My great, great grandfather, David

Rodgers, came to Canal Township in the early 1820s and married Lila Beatty, daughter of the first settler in the area. One of their sons, Robert Rogers, married Emily Emily Rifenberg, and their family lived at Baker Hill near Cooperstown. I understand their thirteen children sometimes were referred to as "Baker's dozen". Several of the children died during a cholera epidemic, leaving only one surviving son, James Henry Rogers, my maternal grandfather born in 1860. Around age sixteen he left home and became an early resident of Galloway.

Chapter 3
1859-1936

This chapter concerns the Galloway I knew primarily through family stories passed on from my maternal grandmother, Ida (McGinnis) Rogers, my mother, my maternal uncle, Robert Wilbur Rogers, and various older Galloway neighbors, most notably Willis J. Frankenberger.

Immediately following the 1859 drilling of the Drake oil well the Galloway area, along with much of northwestern Pennsylvania, was transformed by the "oil excitement". Some financially poor farmers became millionaires overnight by selling or leasing their lands to oil speculators. Many new villages formed, based largely on the needs of oil men and their families. Those near Galloway ranged in size from relatively smaller ones such as Petroleum Center to Pithole. The latter, although in existence only a few years, is said at one time to have been the third largest city in the state.

Among these villages was Fee, the former name for Galloway. It was named after a physician, William M. Fee. Dr. Fee and his father had purchased a large tract of land from a man named Edward Patchell who earlier had purchased it from heirs of William Penn. In addition to his medical practice, Dr. Fee became involved in the oil excitement, drilling his first well in 1871. Due to health concerns he moved from the area to Florida in the 1880s. During the 1884 to 1900 period the village of Fee had its own post office, with A. Dunbar as postmaster (from the book, Pennsylvania Postal History by John Kay and Chester Smith, 1976).

Land deed to William Patchell (1838)

With the coming of the oil rush the physical appearance of the Fee area was transformed. Trees were cleared from much of the land. There were tall wooden derricks at the site of each of the many oil wells which were drilled. Many dirt roads were cut to accommodate well drilling and maintenance equipment, and many small houses were built for persons frequently referred to as "lease" workers and their families. Most of the "lease house" sites had shallow, hand-dug water wells, and small gardens. Cows grazed freely, some reportedly traveling as far as Patchel Run. Their bells could be heard for some distance as they returned in the evening. I understand that around the intersection of present Route 417 and Infield Drive the land was almost completely cleared of trees and underbrush, such that one could see far in all directions. Of course, main roads such as Route 417 were not paved, and often were deep in mud,. At some point during this period a boardwalk from Galloway to what later came to be called the village of Rocky Grove was constructed, making foot traffic easier.

Prominent family names from various decades of those times included Egbert, Fee, Bleakley, Miller, Sibley, Patchel, Redmon, Sanford, Fitzgerald, Aulenbaucker, Harper, Burkhardt, Hodgson, Shealy, Grimm, Lamberton and Grant. Most would have been known to Galloway residents as the wealthy owners who employed them on the extensive nearby oil leases. The Grant name, however, also was well known because during the early part of the 20th century, the family of Joseph Wadsworth Grant had an elegant for the times summer home at the top of Galloway Hill. They named it Colonia, and for at least two decades it was the site of family weddings and frequent parties for members of Franklin's socially elite. After the death of Mrs. J. W. Grant in 1925 the house furnishings were sold and it remained vacant for some time. Perhaps because my grandfather had been a Grant lease employee for many years, my parents were able to rent Colonia. It was our home from 1937 through 1947.

Some detailed description of the Galloway of this period comes from recorded 1973 recollections of my mother. As she told it, her father, James H. Rogers came to work in the oil fields of Fee (Galloway) about 1876 at the age of sixteen. He lived in a rather large boarding house known as the Burton House which was close to the main road, now Route 417. It was on the left hand side of a lane with no known name, but today could be considered a westward extension of Infield Drive if the latter continued across Route 417. There were multiple houses on that lane, including one where the local law enforcement person, Squire Ross, lived. In the late 1870s her father married Nancy Morrison, and in 1880 they had one child, Clifford O. Rogers. Nancy died at a young age which was not uncommon in those days. In 1889 he married Ida McGinnis who had lived at what then was known as McGinnis Hollow on the upper reaches of Patchel Run. While still living in the boarding house they had two children, Robert Wilbur in 1890 and, my mother, Ruth, in 1895. In the late 1890s they moved almost directly across the road to a house then owned by Sam Harper and his wife Jenny. The latter was a teacher and artist, who had her studio immediately behind the house. She is the person credited with having named the village of Rocky Grove. Shortly after the move another child, James. was born. My grandparents lived in that home until their deaths in the 1940s, following which my parents purchased and lived in it. It remained in the family until 1979.

Harper-Rogers home (late 1800s) (view to north from derrick near Infield Drive)

Much of the information I gathered regarding Galloway of the 1860-1900 period came from Willis Frankenberger who related memories of the heyday of the oil fields, the changing appearance of the land, and some of the social life of the times. Regarding the latter, I recall his stories of "old home week" celebrations where persons would come in horse-drawn carriages from nearby villages such as Utica, Hannaville, Cooperstown and Dempseytown for a day of fun and good eating. My then fifteen-year-old's mind and present senior citizen's memory may have distorted some of the details of what he described. However, I recall images of these celebrations as including fiddle music, women in long dresses serving food at a large array of picnic tables, and men with visible-hammer shotguns shooting pigeons released individually from a trap. Other descriptions, stories and anecdotes regarding Galloway life during the early 20th century primarily were from my mother and uncle. Some mentioned below may be of interest to readers.

There were as many as three churches on Galloway during the first half of the twentieth century. One was a Methodist church on the left hand side of present Route 417 at the top of the hill, directly across from the lane leading to Colonia, and approximately across from the present "Village of Galloway" sign. Another was on the right side of the road approximately at the site of the sign. The denomination of the latter was reported by my mother to have been Episcopalian. She recalled that parishioners there often become "quite emotional". That church reportedly burned to the ground sometime in the 1920s. A third church existed for awhile further down hill, approximately across from the later site of the Ralph Moyer home. It was said to be the place of worship of a Kellyite sect.

To the best of my knowledge, during many of the middle years of the 19th century most Galloway school children attended a one-room school near Keely Corners which later was the site of a grange hall. It may have been the one my maternal grandmother told of attending by walking up over the hill from her upper Patchel Run home. It probably was in the early1880s that another school was built on the left hand side of present Route 417 a hundred yards or so before its intersection with Warren Road. By the late 1880s a larger school, initially referred to as the Fee School, was built on the right hand side of Warren road just past that intersection. It accommodated grades one through eight. Students wanting a high school education had to attend school in Rocky Grove. The Fee school closed in 1938, and thereafter all students were bused to Rocky Grove.

Fee school house (late 1800s- early 1900s)
Courtesy of Venango County Historical Society

Recreation by most Galloway residents during the earlier decades of the 20th century often centered around "picture shows" at the two Franklin movie theaters, the Orpheum and the Park. Until the late 1920s these were silent movies. Theatrical productions at the Franklin Opera House also were popular with some. Other recreation included following local baseball teams, picnics in the woods near a spring or stream, gathering and roasting chestnuts in the fall, fishing on the Allegheny River, French Creek or Sugar Lake, and riding the street car from Rocky Grove to the quite-fabulous-for-the-times Monarch Park. That trip involved passing through

Franklin, crossing the Allegheny River on the upper deck of the two-tiered Big Rock Bridge, and proceeding up the Lower Two Mile Run valley to the park. A few residents also were fans of horse racing at Prospect Hill which was near the present Miller-Sibley field.

Galloway had its own baseball team and ball field during the 1910-1925 period, and played teams from Dempseytown and other nearby villages. The field was located approximately 300 yards behind the Methodist Church. My maternal uncles Jim and Wilbur frequently played for the team, and Jim later played for other nearby teams. He gained local fame for his unique catching style which earned him the nickname "one hand Rogers". I often wonder whether Jack Harper, the only major league baseball player from Galloway, ever played on that Galloway field.

Family picnics often were held at Birch Spring located off the left side of present Highway 417 about one half mile beyond the intersection of 417 and Warren Road. While resting in the shade of the large birch tree, baskets of home-cooked bread, spread with home-canned blackberry or raspberry jam and other goodies were washed down with cold, crystal clear water from the spring.

As I understand, the horse racing was sulky only, but involved some high level competition. Some patrons were politically and financially "well-connected". My grandfather, although not one of the latter, participated in some of the racing events. Judging from many pictures in my mother's collection, fishing was very good in those days. Some showed large strings of bass from Sugar Lake; and muskies and walleyes from river, creek and lake were plentiful. A hotel at

Sugar Lake was a favorite getaway site for fisherman, as well as for dating couples who, of course, were chaperoned before marriage. Other such sites were "Takitezy", a small lodge along French Creek, and the many small cottages along that stream which could be accessed by a short train ride from Franklin to Utica with a stop at Takitezy.

Visits to Monarch Park before its closing in 1928 must have been thrilling experiences for most Galloway residents. At a time when very few had electricity or indoor plumbing, this park with its many electric lights, large dance pavilion, merry-go-round, roller coaster, Ferris wheel, bowling alley, and frequent celebrity presentations probably seemed "out of this world" to many.

As with most families, my grandparents had stories to tell of psychic phenomena and various amusing, dangerous, or tragic experiences. Some may be of interest to readers, and may help illustrate Galloway life in the late 19th and early 20th centuries.

A story of paranormal communication involved a maternal great aunt who, in the middle of a Galloway night, awakened to see a short-lived vision of her sister standing at the foot of her bed. The next day news came that the sister had died elsewhere at about the same time. A somewhat similar and amusing story concerned another aunt, Ada (McGnnis) Parshall, who at the time lived in a lease house a couple of hundred yards downhill from Colonia. One night while her husband was working on a nearby well drilling rig she awakened to see what she perceived to be a miniature devil at the foot of her bed. She ran in her nightgown to the rig to tell her husband who then returned with her to the house and discovered a bat in the bedroom. In certain postures bats do have a devilish look, perhaps especially to a half-awake person.

Although panthers, wolves and bears roamed the region during the 18th century, this apparently was not true by the next century. A favorite story passed down through the family was that my grandmother, upon returning home from school to her upper Patchel Run home one evening encountered a large bear. This would have been a very rare event at the time. It reportedly led to her refusing to attend school for awhile. Was this real, or just a good excuse to skip school? The story was sworn to be true even sixty years later.

Although there were rumors of copperheads on the Redmon lease on the far side of Patchel Run, encounters with poisonous snakes at Galloway also were rare in those days. However, once during the late 1800s or early 1900s as my grandmother was accompanying my grandfather while he checked wells on the ridge above the Allegheny River, she stepped over a large rattlesnake. Luckily, the snake was unable to strike. This later was discovered to have been due to its having recently swallowed a rabbit.

Crime apparently was quite rare at the Galloway of those days. Much of the squire's policing work involved subduing and removing hostile drunks.

Nevertheless, my grandfather often told of three events which easily could have led to criminal charges. During his later years of employment with the Grant family he was in a supervisory position and delivered pay to workmen at their various work locations on the oil lease. His dog, Sport, usually accompanied him in the buggy. As they approached a bend on a dirt road at a brisk pace Sport began barking. Grandfather slowed the buggy and stopped immediately in front of a wire which had been strung across the road in an apparent attempt to cause the horse and buggy to wreck and possibly turn over. With Sport in pursuit, two men took off running through the woods. This probably was less out of fear of the dog than of the .32 caliber revolver my grandfather often carried. A second event occurred when during one early morning hour grandfather heard a horse whinnying, grabbed his revolver, looked out his upstairs bedroom window and saw a man walking his favorite horse down his driveway. A single shot toward the sky sent the man running very rapidly down the boardwalk without the horse. The third event occurred when another aunt was home alone while her husband worked a night shift. Hearing a noise, she looked downstairs and saw a strange man approaching the stairs. Thinking quickly she threw a clothes basket filled with heavy irons at him, and yelled to her absent husband "bring the shotgun". The intruder left, and, assuming there really was a gun, I suspect she then armed herself.

Probably the most publicized violent event on Galloway during this period occurred in April of 1922. The version of the event told me by family members differed somewhat from that reported in the Franklin News Herald. Basically what happened was that there were a few friends who sometimes played cards together. Late one evening one of them heard a commotion in his chicken coop, and took his shotgun to the coop to kill or scare off what he thought was a raccoon or other animal after his chickens. Depending on the version of the story, he either fired into the coop accidentally killing one of his card-playing friends who may have been there to steal a chicken, or he was charged by two men running out of the coop, fell, and the gun discharged, accidentally killing the friend. According to the newspaper version, a court composed of local citizens was soon organized to consider facts of the case, and he was exonerated of any crime.

Of course there were other tragedies at Galloway during that period. There were stories of a boy being killed and another losing sight in one eye when they were playing with dynamite. And, a young girl died when her night clothes caught fire from getting too close to an open-flame natural gas stove. Such stoves commonly were used for heating Galloway homes even into the mid 20th century. The earliest telephone systems used by a few residents of Galloway apparently were highly susceptible to lightning strikes, resulting in occasional deaths of persons holding phones during storms.

As noted earlier, there were many oil-related developments in the Galloway region from the 1859 drilling of the Drake well through the remainder of the eighty-year period covered in this chapter.

In the early years of the 1860s it was not uncommon to have some "flowing" wells where oil pushed by underground deposits of natural gas gushed to the surface with no need for pumping. Eaton mentions associated dangers as when the natural gas from one such well on the nearby Buchanan Farm ignited, killing eighteen persons, completely destroying nearby structures, and proving to be very difficult to extinguish. Oilmen soon learned to contain the natural gas, eventually capturing it, storing it, and piping it into homes. Gas lighting and gas stoves began replacing or supplementing candles, oil lamps and coal and wood-burning stoves. Over time, flowing wells became rare and those requiring pumping often had to be drilled increasingly deeper to reach financially profitable quantities of oil. Drilled wells varied widely from "dry holes" to very high producing ones such as the famous "Dolly Varden" at Galloway. An uncle told me that well was located just to the right of the lane leading from Route 417 to Colonia.

Galloway's most famous well (1870s)

During most of the years in this period and beyond it was common practice to drill to a certain depth and then "shoot" or "torpedo" the well by carefully placing a strategic amount of nitroglycerin at the bottom which, when set off, would blast a cavern into which oil could flow. This, it was hoped, would enable a financially profitable reservoir of oil for future pumping. It was a potentially very dangerous enterprise. There were stories of "torpedo men" and their wagons being completely blown apart when nitroglycerin accidentally exploded. Nevertheless, the shooting of a well could be an interesting event, and for many years it was common for Galloway residents to gather at a well site to watch the action. Typically this involved nothing more than a geyser of soil, water and perhaps some oil exploding up to forty feet or so above the surface of the well. It was all over in minutes.

As the years passed and mechanized vehicles became available, the ubiquitous wooden derricks originally needed for housing and using the tools needed for drilling and maintenance of wells began to disappear. The functions of the earlier derricks were replaced by long steel masts trucked in and temporarily erected on-site. Most wells by then did not have a stand-alone pump at each. Multiple wells were pumped at a distance from a central "pump house" using steel cables, often referred to as "rod lines". Each rod line was attached at one end to an individual well's pumping mechanism, and at the other end to a wheel in a central pump house. As I recall, the pumping mechanism consisted of two, four-to-five foot long, 8 by 8 inch wooden beams fastened together in an L shape. The rear of a horizontal bottom beam rested on a large hinge attached to it and to a well-anchored surface below. One end of a rod line was attached near the top of the vertical beam. A pull on the line would tilt the vertical beam backward and simultaneously raise the horizontal beam. The other end of the rod line was attached to a large wheel in a distant pump-house. The wheels were designed to alternate between clockwise and counterclockwise movement. Such movement caused rod lines attached to one side of the wheel to pull on those lines thereby lifting the horizontal beam of the L shaped piece on the other end, while simultaneously lowering beams attached to lines on the other side of the wheel. This rising/lowering resulted in a pumping action via a mechanism attached to the L form at the well. Wells could be a hundred yards or more from their common pump-house. Along that distance rod lines were supported by hooks hung from large wooden posts or from tent-shaped structures constructed from steel pipes. With each rise/fall pumping stroke a mixture of salt water and crude oil was emitted into a small wooden tank beside the well. The salt water would overflow, and the crude oil would remain in the tank until removed by workers. A News Herald article credited J. W. Grant for inventing this widely used pumping system.

Of course with the growth of the oil industry in the region, supportive businesses were established. The Oil Well Supply company in nearby Oil City was a good example, and many local persons were employed there during the latter years of this period. However, it was oil refineries which once employed the majority of Galloway residents who were not "lease workers".

In 1872 what would for awhile be the largest oil refinery in the world, the Eclipse Works, was built along the Allegheny River. It stretched on both sides of present Route 8 from near the French Creek Washington Crossing bridge to beyond the Rocky Grove Front Street intersection. Until its closing in 1937 large numbers of residents of Galloway were employed there. It may be of interest to some readers that oil tank fires were fairly frequent at the Eclipse. My mother recalled the eerie, mournful sound in the night of the Eclipse fire alarm which would be sounded to summon firefighters. Footsteps of those from Galloway could be heard as they ran the mile or so down the boardwalk to Rocky Grove and the refinery.

Another refinery with a long history in the area was the Galena-Signal Oil Company. It became especially well known for the superior quality of its oil used for lubricating railroad signals of the time. During later years it also produced motor oil for automobiles.

An article printed in the August 12th, 1925 edition of the Franklin News Herald may be of special interest to some readers. It describes in some detail a Galloway reunion held in conjunction with an Old Home Week celebration. More than eighty former residents of Galloway met at the Methodist Episcopal Church for what was described as the "most notable program that district ever knew-a time of reminiscence and philosophizing over the departed days". Those listed as present included Frank H. Fee, son of William Fee, as well as many of the persons mentioned in the next chapter.

Chapter 4

Home Sites and Residents
1937-1965

I begin this chapter with a somewhat detailed description of Colonia as I remember it during the ten years we lived there. My earliest Galloway memories were of our family moving into Colonia. Although that Grant summer home had been vacant and relatively neglected for a few years prior to 1937, there remained indications of earlier splendor: a tennis court, a white picket fence on two sides of the property, a large screened-in porch, black, red and yellow raspberry patches, and several huge oak trees. I recall that two of those were within four or five feet of each other with a wooden seat built between them. Another such tree was near the back door on the wide brick sidewalk leading to the driveway. There was a two-step cement structure near the front picket fence gate for ease of stepping out of a vehicle, probably of the horse-drawn type. There was a large chicken coop about thirty yards behind and below the house; and another thirty yards downhill from that building was a combination garage and barn with a hay mow and attached shed for a cow or horse. Of course there were multiple oil wells nearby, at least two within one hundred feet of the house. For some time the pervasive scent of crude oil, and the squeaking sounds emanating from moving, insufficiently lubricated rod-line supports required some getting used to. But, I had my own second floor bedroom with a long range southern view. With my toy telescope I could see cars ascending the "Pittsburgh Road" about two miles away on the other side of Franklin. That made me happy.

Wedding at Colonia (circa 1905) & Jimmie and Judy Evans at Colonia (circa 1941) (Mr. Snyder's horse, and oil well pump and tank in background)

Remaining pages of this chapter provide remembered details of other Galloway residences during these twenty-eight years. They also include some personal observations about individual residents. The detailed descriptions of house locations likely will be of little or no interest to many readers. If so, such readers may wish to skip this section and move on to Chapter 5.

There were were six or seven houses on the left hand side of Route 417 between Rocky Grove and the top of Galloway Hill and one on the right hand side. Families with names such as Kossman, Petersen, Kiskadden, Keith and Turner lived there during at least some of these years. However, I had little contact with most of those families, so will start with two families about whom I have more detailed memory.

About100 yards downhill from the present Village of Galloway sign and on the left side of Route 417 going north was the home of Ralph and Della Moyer, and their children Janet, Jay and "Skip". Jay eventually would become one of my closest childhood friends. Mr. Moyer was remembered by many of us as the friendly man with the photo processing equipment and short wave radio over his garage. He also was the keeper of bob sleds which, on appropriate winter days he would allow the more adventuresome among us to ride down some of the slippery hillside roads of Galloway.

Seventy five yards or so above Moyer's on the left was the home of my earliest childhood friend, Neal Barnes, his mother and his considerably older adult brother. Neal soon moved with his mother to Rocky Grove, but we remained friends into adulthood, occasionally going hunting together. Tragically, and somewhat ironically, he died in 1962 in an automobile accident on a curve of Highway 417 within a hundred or so yards of his early childhood home.

Next on the left at the top of the hill was the home during much of this time of Ellis Free and his wife and children Doris, Gladys, Marjorie, Betty and Jim. Doris was older and Jim considerably younger than I, but the others were frequent playmates during some of my pre-teen years. Betty and I attended the same grades and classrooms for our entire twelve years of school. Later during this time period the home was purchased by Ernest and Eva Mae Montgomery, and that family lived there for many years. I remember Mr. Montgomery as a friendly man. He and his wife were professional bee keepers. I often saw one of their children, Judy, at Galloway when she was a young girl. (She and her husband, Richard Shingledecker, now are owners of the Galloway landmarks, Lucky Hills Golf Course and Dawndi's Restaurant.)

Beside the Free home and immediately before the old Galloway church was a dirt "lease" road leading from Route 417 to the old Galloway ball field mentioned earlier and on to the village of Oak Hill. About 80 yards up that road on the right was a "lease house" occupied in late 1930s/early 1940s by a Lineman family, and then later for over a decade by David Orr, Sr., his wife Rachael and their children David, Jr., Donald (Donnie), Marlyn, and Kay. As a teen-ager and for years later I spent many days hunting and fishing with David and Donnie and their father. David and his wife, Myrna (Rice) Orr became long-time friends to the time of his passing in 2002.

About 100 yards further on that dirt road were remnants of the old Galloway ball field. Another couple of hundred yards beyond that was the home of "Bud" Dolan, and his wife and children, Ivan, Wadsworth ("Wad") and a daughter we called "Sis". In their yard was an open, very large wooden tank containing lukewarm water, apparently part of a cooling system for an engine in a nearby oil well pump house. Whatever its purpose, the Dolan children frequently enjoyed playing in it. One could continue then for a half mile or so to Oak Hill, passing on the left a large field where we picked many huckleberries in season,. That field also was where many residents gathered in the 1940s to watch a small plane snatch a bag of mail suspended between two tall posts for transport to Pittsburgh: the regions first airmail service.

Along much of that road could be found stone walled, partially filled in basements, and remaining fruit trees from multiple small homesteads which had existed there a few decades earlier. I was told that one had been the home of a Wertman family, likely including Sally Wertman who wrote a Galloway news column for the Franklin paper during some years of the early 20th century. All that remained was the basement, and a large apple tree which still produced very tasty golden apples.

Returning now to highway 417, one would find the white Methodist Episcopal church on the left, and across the road from it, the entrance to the lane leading to Colonia, mentioned earlier as the Grant summer home rented by my parents from 1937 to 1947.

On the left hand side and another estimated 80 yards beyond the church was a lease house occupied for a few years by a Huff family. That family included a son, Willis, of about my age who died during the Korean War. Later it was occupied by a Brown family including children Bill and Glenna Rae who were occasional friends during pre- and early teen-age years. During part of the 1950s it was occupied by Leo McCarren and family.

This "virtual tour" leads now to what I like to refer to as the "heart of Galloway", i. e., the intersection of Route 417 with what is now known as Infield Drive to the right (east) and another shorter dirt road to the left (west). Many of us in the period being covered here knew those roads as Frankenberger Lane and Jacoby Lane respectively, family names of persons whose homes were there. As mentioned earlier, the road to the west once had been the site of a large boarding house, as well as the home of "Squire Ross" and a few other homes including that of my maternal great grandmother Mary (Sauer) McGinnis who died in 1912. However, by the 1930s there was only one home on the road. It was occupied from the 1940s by "Toby" and Ruth Jacoby and their children Joan, Henry, Donnie, Gracie, Judy and Barbie. Joan and I attended many of the same elementary and high school classes, and both graduated in 1951. Henry and I became close buddies for most of our childhood and early teen-age years, often going hunting together, and roaming the woods around Colonia and Patchel Run. He had excellent visual-motor skills, and could throw a penny in the air, then aim a .22 rifle and usually hit the coin. It was a feat I envied! Such visual-motor integration skills undoubtedly played a role in his many later successes as a champion stock car racer at nearby Tri-City Speedway.

"Daredevil" Henry Jacoby (circa 1945) (suspended
10 feet up on swing hanger)

I spent many hours at the always-welcoming Jacoby home. Many of those were in Mr. Jacoby's garage where he and Henry taught me the functions of crankshafts, camshafts, transmissions, and differentials, or "rear ends" as mechanics of the time often called them. Donnie and I also occasionally hunted together, but he and his sisters Gracie and Judy were younger, and thus we shared fewer interests and time together. Sadly, Barbie the youngest Jacoby child became ill, and passed away at a very young age.

Returning now to 417, but turning right (East) on Infield Drive one would first have come to the home of Willis and Maude Frankenberger. As children, my sister Judy and I often walked a few steps up the driveway of that house as we made our way from Colonia up to our "Grandma's house". I recall Mr. Frankenberger as a friendly man who kept several bee hives, maintained a small vegetable garden, and had an interesting old double-barreled shotgun with "rabbit ears" (exposed hammers). As noted, he was the one who told me tales of late 19th century Galloway. After the passing of Willis and Maude, his grandson Jim and wife Zana, and their daughters moved into the house. Jim and I were frequent hunting partners during the 1960s.

Next on the left side of Infield Drive was the home of Charles Snyder, and his wife and family. Most referred to Mr. Snyder as "Charlie". He was a friendly, very hard working, thin, but very strong man. He was employed at times by Sugarcreek Township, performing chores such as manually loading and throwing ashes onto icy roads from the bed of a truck during Galloway's many winter snow and ice storms. He plowed gardens with a horse which often grazed in the field between his house and Colonia which was located about 80 yards from the Snyder home directly across Infield Drive. Occasionally he was hired to prepare new sites for the many outhouses which existed on Galloway, or to help during local moves by using his horse to pull a type of "sled" on which furniture and other objects had been placed. As an elementary school child I recall playing ("rough-housing") in the field with his daughters Esther and Doris and other neighborhood children. This was especially memorable because they, being a little older, out-weighed me and invariably could "pin me down".

About seventy yards further on the left was the home of Ernest and Mabel Frankenberger, and children Ernest, Jr., Jim, Helen, and Betty. The latter two, being closest to my age, were school classmates for several years. Mr. Frankenberger was a World War I veteran who, as I understood, had suffered lung damage from poison gas, and was partially disabled. I recall his serving as the local air-raid warden during World War II. During the time period covered here that was the last house on Infield Drive for about another two hundred yards. Along that stretch were several points of special interest to a bicycling pre- and early-teen such as myself. These included a large steel pipe under the road through which passed a moving rod-line for pumping a distant oil well, a small swampy area on the right where some teens attempted ice skating during winter months, and some wintergreen berry patches with tasty fruit in season. Several small dirt or grass-covered lease roads branched off from the main road. These invited exploration whether on foot, by bicycle, on horseback or via dirt bikes. Horseback riders needed to exercise much caution when passing over the pipe since some horses apparently perceived the moving rod-line as a snake, and would bolt. It was common to see deer, and to flush grouse along these roads.

At the end of the road were two lease houses, home to different families over the course of this period. However, most of my memories are of the house on the left occupied by Ralph Cheers, his wife Katherine and children Peggy, Raymond and Ronnie. Many enjoyable days were spent there and in the woods nearby. Activities included swinging on a swing attached to the limb of a large tree in the front yard, playing ball in the small field nearby, or playing "commandos" in the woods and blind man's bluff in the yard. Raymond became one of my closest childhood friends, and was a classmate for all twelve of our school years. Mr. and Mrs. Cheers always were welcoming. I assume that Mr. Cheers once had been an oil lease employee. However, he later was an auto mechanic for the Brecht Chevrolet dealership in Franklin, and became known as the best Chevrolet mechanic in the region. Often he would hurry home for a quick lunch. I remember well the cloud of dust his black 1938 Chevrolet produced on Infield Drive as he drove from Highway 417 to home. I recall asking him once if he didn't worry about having to make a quick stop. He smiled and replied, "I can stop on a dime, and have nine cents change!"

But, the house on the right also elicits many memories. For most of these years it was occupied by Duke and Kate Rosenberg. As with the Cheers, they always were welcoming. And Duke, whom I recall preferred that name to being called Mr. Rosenberg, always had interesting stories to tell. For me, the most interesting of these concerned dogs, animals and hunting. He was an avid raccoon hunter, and, at least by his account, usually had the best dogs in the area. One Duke memory is of seeing a groundhog run across the road in front of my bicycle. Somehow this one looked different, so I stopped to describe it to Duke who assured me it was a "whistle pig". Not realizing at the time that this was simply an alternate term for a woodchuck, I left thinking I had just seen a rare species of animal. A few years later, around age fourteen, when walking with my friend Henry Jacoby along Patchel Run, we encountered an animal which looked to us like a medium-sized brown bear with a raccoon-like tail. Being in a quite isolated area, we hurried away, and I went to my woods-wise friend Duke for advice. He assured me no bears had been seen in the area for many years, and certainly none with ring tails. However, he patiently consulted wildlife books to see if we could find any such animal, perhaps one which had escaped from a zoo. We had no luck. So, I moved on, still wondering what the unusual animal possibly could have have been. I figured that it must have been a very exotic one, because it was a mystery, even to Duke. My father, however, had a much simpler explanation. He noted that about two miles away a Dr. Nordstrom raised very large, black Newfoundland dogs, and one may have mated with a brindle German shepherd, resulting in this mystery animal. Whatever the case, it was years before I returned to that area without my trusty rifle.

Duke and Kate later built a home a couple of miles from the center of Galloway on White Temple Hill, and, as an adult I still enjoyed stopping by to hear a few Duke stories. The last time was during the 1960s. It was deer season, and he was confined to a wheelchair. As he told it, early one morning he heard about five shots "up on the old Reeser place", and told Kate to open a window and bring his rifle. Within minutes a buck came running through his side yard and he fired through the open window. Although Kate believed he missed it, he said, "just wait a few minutes and go down the hill and look". Sure enough, she soon returned with the news that there soon would be venison on their table. I believe that was the last time I saw Duke.

Returning now to Highway 417 and turning right (north) there were twelve houses before coming to the intersection of 417 and Warren Road.

A side yard of the first house on the left adjoined "Jacoby Lane". It was occupied for most years of this period by Roy Smith and his wife Belle. I recall them as a friendly older couple of retirement age who kept their beautiful and spacious house and yard in immaculate condition. After they moved to be closer to their children in a nearby town, the house was occupied for some time by Roy Lusher, and his wife Priscilla (Keith) Lusher, and later by Ken and Beverly (Brady)Young and children Dick, Mona and Kelly. However, I believe the latter family may have moved there shortly after the period being covered here.

Motorcyclists Wilbur and Ruth Rogers in front of
Belle and Roy Smith home (circa 1915)

Next, and very close by on that side of Route 417 was the home of Curt and Alice Keith, and their children. I remember names of four of the children: Ardythe (aka "Tiny"), Eleanor, Marilyn, and Shirley. The one closest to my age was Shirley. As I recall, Mr. Keith worked on an oil lease. Mrs. Keith was well known by neighborhood children for her periodic taffy-making events during which many of us would be invited to come and enjoy a sweet treat.

Next door was the large, impressive home of William Hodgson, and his wife TeMoy. I recall visiting there with my grandmother who was a friend of Mrs. Hodgson, and enjoying glasses of delicious grape juice. According to information found in his obituary, Mr. Hodgson's father, George W. Hodgson and wife had owned and lived in that home until their deaths in 1923. He had been quite financially successful, and was very influential in the early history of Galloway. One of his daughters, Annalena, became a teacher in the Rocky Grove Schools. She was the first grade teacher of my two sisters and myself. Apparently a portion of that house once had housed an office of Dr. William Fee for whom the area originally was named. This was told to me by my mother who said that, as a young child playing with a friend in a room of the house circa 1900 she had observed various medical instruments and supplies. She was told they had belonged to Dr. Fee. By the 1950s the Hodgsons had died, and various others lived in the house. The only one I recall was Rial Schaffer in the 1960s.

A few yards further on the left was a house which I believe was for awhile the home of Wallace and Lucy Keith and children Grace, Lloyd, Virgil, Dick and Stella (aka "Snookie"). However, for most of the years that I knew that family they lived in a newer house next door, and a Bower family resided in the older home. Lloyd Keith died unexpectedly in his thirties, apparently of a heart condition. I never knew him other than as one of the older boys on our school bus. Virgil was slightly older than I, but we interacted occasionally. I recall him mainly as a handsome, strong and athletic teenager who could dive gracefully from the diving board at a local playground swimming pool, and readily hit home-runs at our high school softball field. Although friendly, many of us thought of him as someone you wouldn't want to "mess with". Dick and Snookie were younger than I. As with their parents, I would recognize them in passing, but there was little interaction.

I am not certain, but I believe the next house on the left side was owned and occupied for most of these years by an elderly woman named Hannah Brown. Her husband apparently was deceased, and she lived alone. My mother, although a few years younger than Mrs. Brown, often visited her during the 1950s. She was somewhat dependent on neighbors to help out as she attempted to maintain her house and yard. I occasionally mowed her lawn for fifty cents. That was below the going rate at the time, but she believed it was adequate given that she earlier had paid only a quarter. I recall her as a friendly, positive and somewhat jolly person. After she passed, the Parquette family, Tom, Della, and son Ralph moved into the home. Mrs. Parquette and my mother became very good friends. After my Father's passing in 1964 the Parquette family, along with the Ken Young family mentioned earlier, became major sources of support for my mother for the following fifteen years.

I understood from my mother that during the middle 1800s there had been a school on the site of the seventh and final house on the left side of the road. For several years, perhaps even into the middle to late 1940s, the owners and occupants of a house at that site were Port Smith and his wife.

I recall that a Mrs. Story and her son John lived there during the 1950s. John died in a tragic auto accident near the town of Reno circa 1954.

Of course there are a great many memories of the first of the five houses on the _right_ side of that short stretch of highway 417 between Infield Drive and Warren Road. I understand that the site on which it stood was one of several parcels of land sold by Edward Patchell from his original much larger purchase mentioned in Chapter 3. He sold it to a man named Sam Harper and his wife Jenny in the late 1870s or early 1880s. They built a house on it, and in 1898 (as also mentioned in Chapter 3) sold it and about seven acres of land to my maternal grandfather, James Henry Rogers. Later he sold approximatcly two acres on the eastern side, and proceeded to clear the remaining acres. Eventually he transformed them into a mini-farm replete with a two-story barn where a horse and a cow resided, a large chicken coop, an apple orchard, and fields where corn, sweet potatoes and various other vegetables and strawberries were grown. Much of his produce was sold at the farmers' curb market in Franklin. When purchased, the lot also held a small outbuilding which Mrs. Harper [Jenny (Braden) Harper] used as her art studio. Later my grandparents installed water pipes and used it as a "wash house". I recall a "wringer" washer, ironing boards and various tubs and scrubbing boards being housed there. A pumphouse, which my grandfather referred to as a "powerhouse", also was built on the land. It housed an engine which, via rod-lines, enabled the pumping of several once moderately profitable oil wells he had drilled on the land. During his later years the powerhouse was used largely as what today might be considered his "man-cave". Until the late 1950s it housed a single cylinder gas engine for pumping water via a rod-line and oil well type pumping system. Water was pumped from a shallow well in the southeastern corner of the land to a storage tank on the hill above the house. This arrangement supplied household water until the early 1970s when a deep well was drilled a few feet above the house.

Rogers home (1920s)

Many memories remain of "grandma and grandpas' house" from preschool age to their deaths in the mid-1940s. Pre-school examples include gathering eggs with grandpa who would give me a quarter if I found a "double-yoker", and watching him set off in the backyard large batches of fireworks on the Fourth of July. The latter occurred only prior to 1939 when Pennsylvania banned their sale. Other memories include snuggling up in bed with grandma during overnight visits, and sitting on her lap as she read to me. The latter often occurred as we watched for the occasional car coming up Route 417 and wondering if it would be my parents coming to pick me up.

James H. Rogers and horse "May" (circa 1910) &
Ida V. (McGinnis) Rogers (circa 1910)

Natural gas, oil lamps and lanterns were used for illumination until 1932 when the house was wired for electricity. A couple of gas lights remained in the house for several years, and I recall sometimes coaxing my grandparents to turn off the electricity and light them "just for fun". Until 1962 when a gas furnace was installed, all of the house except the kitchen was heated by open-flame gas stoves. For several years the kitchen contained a wood-burning cook stove. It was replaced by a gas stove circa 1937. Prior to the 1950s the majority of Galloway homes, including this one, had no indoor bathroom. Some jokingly referred to them as having "two (or three or four) bedrooms and a path". But, that was not funny when winter temperatures dropped below freezing!

After my grandfather's death in 1947 my parents purchased the home and land, and it was where my younger sister Judy and I spent our teen-age and early adult years. My older sister, Margie had many fond memories of her grandparents and that house, but by 1947 she was in college, and never actually lived there.

Proceeding north on 417 from the Rogers/Evans house on the right there were about 150 yards of field and a woodlot belonging to the aforementioned Roger's farm. Next there was a relatively new house built, I believe, in the late 1940s. It was occupied by Louis Phillips, his wife and children Louis, Jr., Phyllis, and Andy. Mr. Phillips, as I recall, owned and operated heavy construction equipment, and at least one school bus which he housed in a large garage beside the house. I was in their home on a few occasions, but did not know them well. I do recall Louis, Jr. being a rather "tough-talking" boy whom I always feared. That is, until once I happened by chance to see him shortly after my discharge from the Army when I could bench press 260 pounds. The fear was gone! Phyllis and I attended some high school classes together, and I occasionally saw her at class reunions. Andy was a few years younger. I knew him mainly as one of Henry Jacoby's chief competitors at Tri City Speedway. I don't recall exactly when, but the Phillips family moved to a new home in Rocky Grove, and George and Doris (Free) Cheers bought this property.

Within a few yards further there was a house and lot where a Burk family lived. I believe it had been in the family for some time. During the late 1930s Galloway's only store was on that site. I have heard it referred to as Burk's store. There was a gas pump in front which Dom Spezialy recalled his family using to buy gasoline for their early farm equipment. He believes they sold White Rose gasoline and oil. I went inside the store at least once with my grandparents, and recall it being very small, but well stocked with products. Those included a favorite of mine: small wax bottle-shaped containers filled with colorful "pop", the local term for soft drinks. Dom said the store was destroyed by fire in 1939 or 1940. Although I could not find definite evidence, there was some indication that this site also had been the location of the old Fee Post Office during the late 1800s. For most of the period being covered in this chapter a Burk family lived in the home. I don't recall meeting the parents, and only knew names of two young Burk boys, Jimmie and Charles.

Close by, and next in this sequence of homes was one occupied for many years by Boyd Frankenberger and his wife Evelyn. Mr. Frankenberger, a tall, imposing figure of a man, had served in World War I, attaining the rank of lieutenant colonel. He was an older brother of Ernest Frankenberger mentioned earlier. His wife was a nurse who apparently served as a mid-wife at times. I was told that she was present at my birth. Their home and extensive surrounding acreage once had been owned by a prominent early Galloway resident named Andrew Fitzgerald who had bought it from Edward Patchell. After the Fizgeralds left the home, and prior to the Frankenberger purchase it had been rented briefly by others. Renters included my parents who lived there for a few months in the early 1920s.

The next hundred or so yards on the right was open field for most of this time period, having once been part of the Fitzgerald estate, but purchased during the early 20th century by Vincent Spezialy. I believe it was in the mid-to-late 1960s that a Westover family purchased a lot and had a home on that site. I remember it especially because one of the Westovers was a young boy named Craig who later in the 1970s frequently rode with my son Kent as part of the "Galloway dirt bike gang".

At the end of this strip of land was a house which prior to the Spezialy purchase had for some time been the home of a Jones family. One of the Jones children, Laura, was married to my maternal uncle Wilbur. All of my memories of that house during the 1937-1965 period involved the Spezialy family and the 65 or so acres they owned and farmed. They had a very strong work ethic, raised dairy cows and pigs, and grew fields of corn and hay to sell and to feed the livestock. Mr. and Mrs. Spezialy always made me feel welcome, and I was allowed to roam freely over their acreage to hunt groundhogs, crows, grouse and deer.

Dom Spezialy "young man on the farm" (circa 1950)

Above the Spezialy home and barn were twin peaks. These were prominent, flat topped hills, and two of the highest points in Venango County. I recall that on a couple of occasions as a teenager I worked with several of the Spezialy children to help clear small rocks from the level area on the top of the northernmost of those peaks. The Spezialy family was preparing it to be suitable for planting of crops. It was common to find flint arrow heads there, suggesting that it once was a site of bow and arrow target practice for native Americans. On the sloping sides of this hill there were at least two springs. One on the northeast side had a small cement enclosure which probably once served as a place where horses, cows or deer could go for a drink. Another on the east slope supplied water to the lease houses at the end of Infield Drive. The slopes as well as the edges of the level top, had a large population of groundhogs, leading some of us to refer to the entire hill as "Groundhog Hill". By the late 1950s several of the Spezialy children had moved from the area, including several who went to Alaska. The land continued to be actively farmed for awhile, but sometime after the passing of Mr. Spezialy in 1971 the land was purchased by Mr. and Mrs. Shingledecker who transformed much of it into the Lucky Hills golf course. On that level space at the top of Groundhog Hill is a beautiful log lodge housing Dawndi's Restaurant with great food, service and views. Having visited there several times, I can attest to that. But, I have yet to see groundhog stew on the menu!

For me as a child "Galloway" essentially ended where Highway 417 intersects Warren Road. However, some earlier residents and most residents today would disagree. They probably would extend boundaries at least as far as the top of White Temple Hill on the Warren Road, and at least as far north on Route 417 as its intersection with the present Seysler Road, then right on Sysler to Warren Road. That would include the site of the present Methodist-Episcopal Church of Galloway and all sites within the triangle of land formed by those three roads.

In fact, some might argue that the Galloway boundaries on 417 extend north to what is referred to as Keely Corners and the site of the "red brick house". The latter is a local landmark from the days when brick homes were rare in the area. They could point out that one of the region's earliest school houses and the Galloway Grange Hall were located there. I remember the Grange as a place to go at times to vote in elections, and at other times to enjoy buckwheat cake and sausage dinners offered for various fund-raising purposes. Below I mention briefly some of my memories of homes and people from such an "extended Galloway".

Starting with Warren Road, on the right side was the Fee schoolhouse built in the early 1890s, and closed in 1938. The site was on the Fitzgerald estate, and later owned by the Spezialy family. Students attended there from 1st through 8th grades. Some years after its closing it was converted into a residence and rented by various families. A Grossman family with children named Carl and Freda, and a Barnes family with children named Judy and Jimmy lived in two houses located immediately beyond the school house. Within that same stretch of road, a Girt family had lived for many years in a house where, during the 1940s a Fuller family resided. I interacted some with one of the Fuller children named Carl. A Mr. Krepp and his daughter also lived along that stretch of road. There may have been other family members, but, if so, I never met them. I do recall that in summer months Mr. Krepp would pick large buckets of blackberries, and sell them door-to-door. He also would tell tales of seeing and catching poisonous snakes, especially when he picked berries in the Two Mile Run region. Some doubted the truth of at least some of his stories until one day he came by carrying a pail of berries in one hand and a bag containing a live rattlesnake in the other.

I believe that next on that side of the road was open land, and then the home and barn owned by Joseph Schiffer, his wife Bertha and children, Coleen and Eileen (twins), Ruth, Peggy, and Joe. The Schiffer family was well known for their food store on 13th Street in Franklin which housed a walk-in size freezer where meat could be stored circa 1945-1965. I recall that they also had one of the first, if not the very first, television sets at Galloway. Neighbors and friends often went to watch early programs on this "new" phenomena. It probably was during the 1946-1948 period, with a nine inch set, and Pittsburgh the only channel available. They also had cows, sold Golden Guernsey brand milk, and had some thoroughbred horses. Their daughter Peggy and my sister Judy became best of friends through mutual interests in horses. Judy and Peggy kept in touch for many years.

I believe that next there was a house where one of the Schiffer girls, Ruth, and her husband lived for part of this time. And next to it there was a house where a Confer family lived. Near that site a driveway to the right led 100 yards or so to a house where the family of Sam and Grace Lowry lived for awhile in the 1950s. I didn't know either of those two families, but do recall a boy named "Deb" Confer, and a girl named Mary Lowry. Both attended Rocky Grove schools.

Beyond the Confer home on the right hand side was a group of houses occupied by families whose children also attended Rocky Grove schools, and we occasionally met in classes or on the playground. Family names included Clark, Dolby, Paden, Haggerty, and Ross. Rhoenia (Haggerty) Paden and I were in the same high school graduating class, and sometimes shared memories at class reunions. Bonnie Ross also was a class member, and was another with whom I kept in touch for many years via reunions.

One of Bonnie's siblings was Bob ("Red") Ross. I didn't know him well until after the period of time being covered here, but do recall that during our school days he had a reputation for having a hot temper. I came to know him quite well in the 1970s after he had purchased and moved into Colonia. His son Bob, Jr. and my son Kent had mutual interests in trail bike riding. Red was very mechanically adept, and helped keep our sons' bikes in repair. If one of their bikes would break down at some remote woods location he would ride to their rescue on a four-wheel vehicle he had built and referred to as a "hoopie". As an adult I never saw any indications of hot temper.

There were few houses on the left hand side of Old Warren Road between its intersection with route 417 and White Temple Hill. The first 100 to 200 yards were part of the John Burkhardt farm, and about mid-way in that stretch of land were a large farmhouse and dairy barn. Many persons, including my family, would go there to buy fresh milk.

Neighboring that farm was acreage and a large house with an impressive entry drive owned by Guy Harper and family. There were two daughters, Gloria and Nancy. The Mr. Harper I remember was employed at a Franklin bank, possibly the owner or manager. Otherwise, I have no knowledge of that property or family.

I believe that next door to the Harper home was the home of Emma Siefer, who had been a friend of my maternal grandmother. I recall that after she died in 1970 at the age of 104, my mother, first wife and daughter attended an auction of some of her property.

I have no memories of other homes which may have been on either side of that road. However, I recall that a Kunkle family was well known in that general area for many years, and must have had a home there.

Return now to the 417/ Warren Road junction as I describe memories of an "expanded Galloway" proceeding north on 417 toward Dempseytown. On the left side of the road for 100 to 200 yards there was partially wooded land belonging to the Spezialy farm. At the end of that stretch there was a house and various structures involved in activities of the Thompson Saw Mill. I don't recall ever meeting the owners of the mill, but am quite certain that one of the Schiffer twins mentioned earlier was married to a Thompson. After that there were no structures along that side of the road to its intersection with the present Seysler Road.

On the right side of 417 there were at least 200-300 yards of fields and woods belonging to the Burkhardt Farm, then nothing but woods until midway up what many called Brown Hill. There a home was built circa 1950, but I never knew the owners. Past that point there were only fields as far as Seysler Road.

Chapter 5

Social and Cultural Life
1937-1965

This largest chapter of the book describes everyday life on Galloway in regard to matters such as employment, transportation, education, medical facilities, religion, recreation, and unique mannerisms. It covers a time span of twenty-eight years during which many socio-cultural changes occurred nationwide, and the author grew from childhood to adulthood. Much of what is described centers around the author's perceptions and recollections of personal experiences concerning Galloway life of those times. Therefore, it will not be a completely unbiased description of the culture of Galloway, or of other cities or villages of this period. However, it is likely that older readers who lived at Galloway and surrounding areas will relate to much of the content of the chapter.

Employment

The years from 1937 to 1940 were part of the Great Depression. Yet, according to my mother, Galloway was not nearly as adversely affected as most of the nation. There seemed to be employment on the nearby oil leases for most who wanted work. Although the closing of the Eclipse Works refinery in 1937 must have been a blow to some families, apparently other oil industry-related jobs remained plentiful. Factories in nearby Franklin such as the Chicago Pneumatic Tool Company (CPT) and the Rolling Mill and Foundry Company (later Borg-Warner; Franklin Steel) also offered employment opportunities. I understand that only a very few Galloway families took advantage of the Works Progress Administration (WPA) or other government programs of the Roosevelt administration credited with helping the country get through the Depression years.

My father, Eldridge Dewitt Evans, moved from Alabama to Pennsylvania circa 1920. Due to his origins some local persons referred to him as "Bam". During the depression years he had multiple jobs. He worked at the "rolling mill" in Franklin, and he and my mother raised, boarded and cared for dogs. Regarding the latter, there were no licensed veterinarians in the immediate region for many years, and he began providing services such as grooming dogs, docking tails, inoculating for rabies and other diseases, and euthanizing when seriously ill and considered incurable. When confronted with especially difficult cases, or when surgery was indicated he would take the dog to a licensed veterinarian in Meadville or Union City for treatment. He essentially functioned as a sort of veterinarian's assistant, and at times was referred to by local residents as "the dog man". Most Galloway residents considered their dogs to be "working animals" for hunting rabbits, squirrels or raccoon. They usually kept them outdoors in small kennels. However, many of the wealthier and influential residents of the region treated their dogs more as family members, and were my dad's main customers. A story circulated that when a licensed veterinarian finally moved to the area and threatened to charge dad with practicing veterinary without a license, he was boycotted by these customers. The "real" vet apparently then agreed not to pursue the case and essentially to "live and let live". Dad was still treating dogs until his death in 1964.

As the depression years came to a close with the beginning of World War II, there was full employment for area men (and women) in the military, at specialized munitions companies, and at local factories and oil refineries such as the "Fo Co" (later, Amalie) and Wolf's Head. For many years after the war local residents had many job opportunities, often earning high wages, and considerable vacation time associated with union bargaining power. Factories such as the CPT, and the Joy Manufacturing Company in Franklin were "booming". Canadian fishing trips, new cars every couple of years, and in-ground swimming pools were among the fruits of the labor of many residents, including some from Galloway. Lucrative retirement packages led many workers to make plans to retire in Florida. However, by the end of the twenty-eight year period covered in this chapter the local oil fields had closed, and sporadic lay-offs were occurring in the factories. Some companies were eyeing cheaper labor, often in southern states. The pre-1965 employment picture soon would be changing.

Transportation.

By 1937 it would have been very rare to see a horse and wagon on the highway. Although a few Galloway residents walked to work in Franklin, or to Rocky Grove where they could get a bus to Franklin, nearly all families owned a car. Throughout this entire time period the vast majority of local cars were American made, with Chevrolets, Fords and Plymouths being most common at Galloway. The wealthier families of Franklin usually owned Packards, Cadillacs, or LaSalles; some even had chauffeurs. There were other less commonly seen makes as I once learned when, as a curious fourteen year-old, I walked around Franklin streets taking inventory of car makes. In addition to the above-mentioned ones, I noted Pontiacs, Mercurys, De Sotos, Nashs, Oldsmobiles, Buicks, Lincoln Zephers, Hudsons, Dodges, Studebakers and even a Franklin and a few Model A Fords. Soon the occasional Kaiser, Fraser, Henry J, and Willys would be added to the list.

Cars of those years were very different from today. I had never ridden in a car with an automatic transmission until shortly after World War II. Until then, and for a couple of decades later, most of us drove "stick shift" cars, with "three (or four) on the floor" (referring to the several gear positions a driver could shift into via a lever mounted on the floor). By the late 1940s many cars had the shift lever mounted on the steering column, leading some to refer to that arrangement as "three on the tree". Power steering was not common until at least the mid-1950s. Many young drivers expedited turning of the steering wheel by attaching a "spinner knob" on the wheel, a practice some considered dangerous and frowned upon by police.

It wasn't until the late 1930s that most cars had hydraulic brakes. Prior to that braking was accomplished mechanically via "brake rods" under the car activated by foot pedal pressure at one end, and at the other end pressing brake shoes against a brake drum at each wheel. Unless rods were kept in equal adjustment for all four wheels, applying the brake pedal could cause the car to veer to the left or right. This could be quite dangerous, especially on the icy roads of winter. Some 1930s cars had no heater or radio as standard equipment. After-market radios often were installed, and it was not uncommon for owners to decorate their aerials with squirrel or raccoon tails. Some after-market heaters involved encasing a car's exhaust manifold in a hollow steel shell. As the car moved, air would be captured by a funnel-like apparatus attached to the front of the shell, and would become heated as it moved across the engine's exhaust manifold. The heated air then passed out the rear of the shell and into the car via a hose attached to a hole in the car's floorboard. With such "manifold heaters" fumes from a leaking exhaust manifold could have fatal results. Safety glass was not used in cars during much of this period, some car doors opened from front to back, and seat belts and padded dash boards were not standard in cars until the 1960s. Amazing that most of us survived!

Perhaps the survival rate was due largely to the facts that traffic was light in those days, many cars' top speeds were 70 to 75 mph, and, at least by the late 1940s, the Pennsylvania State Police strictly enforced a 50 mph speed limit. For much of this pre-radar period, police were required to clock a car's speed for at least a quarter mile before writing a speeding ticket. This led many young male drivers, especially, to keep one eye on the road and one on the rear view mirror. I personally recall several times when, upon glancing into my mirror, an officer was so close he appeared to be riding in the back seat.

My family owned two cars during the earlier years of this period, a 1935 two-door Ford and a plum-colored four door 1937 Ford. The latter endured until the 1950s, and was the one with which I learned to drive. My grandfather owned a green 1934 five-window, V8 Ford coupe with a rumble seat which he had driven only 5,600 miles by the time of his death in 1947. During the World War II years when no cars were being produced, there were many knocks on his Galloway door by persons wanting to purchase it. My sister Margie bought it in 1947 and in 1950 gave it to me, providing quite a boost to my high school social life. Although I often regret it, I sold it three years later. On the other hand, it had a manifold heater, mechanical brakes, and no safety glass or seat belts, and I might not be writing this today had I kept it!

Many local boys and young men of the late 1940s and later, including myself, dreamed of owning and "hot-rodding" or "hopping-up" a car as they read about in magazines such as "Hot Rod". However, most could not afford a car, or have the money to purchase such expensive things as dual carburetors. Many dreamed of owning, for example, a 1949 Olds 88 which could hit 100 mph or more on the Pennsylvania Turnpike. I never knew anyone locally who managed that. A few, however, installed "Smitty" mufflers, and shaved the engine heads of their cars to add some horsepower. By the early 1960's several local young men, including a few from Galloway, built "souped-up" cars for dirt track racing as nearby tracks were opened.

By 1937 Route 417 was paved, but there were still many dirt roads, including Warren Road and Seysler Road. For a reason once explained to me, but now forgotten, local dirt roads usually developed a washboard-like surface. This made for a rough ride unless one was moving at a sufficiently high speed, such as 40 mph or higher. Many of us learned to do that to make rides more comfortable for driver and passengers. Later in this 1937-1965 period most roads were "black-topped", and such tactics were not necessary.

Winter driving has always been rather treacherous in the area with its many curves and steep hills when roads become covered with snow and ice. In the earlier years of this period cinders from coal-burning furnaces of homes and factories often were placed at strategic locations at the tops of hills such as Galloway Hill. When a snowfall began, ashes were loaded manually on trucks and spread on the steep portions of roads. Despite such efforts most former Galloway residents will recall being stuck on hills. Many experienced dangerous episodes of skidding on icy spots, sometimes sliding in 180 degree circles. Some drivers used tire chains for many of the winter months. Later, salt was spread manually or mechanically from large trucks to melt ice. While this decreased accidents and the need for chains, it led to rusted auto bodies, and made it necessary to replace exhaust systems every year or two. By the 1960s "snow tires" with thick treads and some with embedded metal studs were common on local cars during winter months.

Before ending this section on automobile transportation it should be noted that throughout most of these years it was quite easy, and safe, to go from place to place by hitch-hiking. For example, once during our early teen-age years Henry Jacoby and I hitch-hiked about fifty miles to Edinboro where my older sister was a college student. And, during the mid-1950s while a student at Clarion College, if my car pool ride was not ready to go when I was, I simply walked to the main street and "thumbed a ride" home. I often gave rides to hitch-hikers, including sometimes at night. As best I can recall, however, it was only men and boys who hitch-hiked locally.

Not all transportation was via automobile during this period. From 1937 until shortly after World War II passenger train service was available in the region. The Erie, Pennsylvania and New York Central lines each had a station in Franklin. Based on what I was told by my mother, relatively few Galloway residents traveled long distance by train; their much more common train travel was across the very few miles on the Erie to Takitezy or Utica for vacation time at cottages "up the crick". And, that was only early in the century prior to most families having automobiles. Such was not the case, however, for persons from wealthy families in the region who into the 1940s often traveled long distances by train for business or pleasure, or to make ship or plane connections for long distance travel.

My few area train memories include my father taking me to see a large train at the Eclipse refinery circa 1937. As I recall, a track followed for some distance the mid-line of present Route 8. As our car pulled along the side of a locomotive which dwarfed our car, it emitted large amounts of steam, and the whistle blew. It must have seemed a fire-breathing dragon to me, and certainly made a lasting impression. The sounds of steam engine whistles in the night were common during the 1937 to mid-1940s period and traveled up and over the hills to places like Galloway. Another memory is of New York Central trains moving down 14th Street in Franklin in front of my great aunt Ada Parshall's home at the corner of Buffalo Street, and moving so slowly that I could reach out and touch them. Sometime in the early to mid- 1950's a "father-son" train trip to Cleveland for an Indian's baseball game was arranged by a Franklin group. Dad and I made the day-long trip on the Erie railroad. It may have been the last of the passenger train trips from that station.

Commercial air travel during the earliest years of this period essentially did not exist in the region. I recall there being a small airport near Galloway, on or very near the Al McElhaney farm. I believe it accommodated only single engine private planes. As children we knew it as a place for the curious to go to see small planes taking off, flying overhead and landing. Through the 1940s and 1950s one had to travel to Pittsburgh or Cleveland to catch a commercial flight. Then, early in the 1960s an airport was established in Franklin serviced by Allegheny Airlines, with connections in Pittsburgh to a great many destinations.

Education.

Galloway children from 1st through 8th grade level attended the old Fee school described earlier until the 1939-1940 school year when a new Rocky Grove School was opened for grades 1 through 12. There was no local public kindergarten during most of these years. Beginning with the 1939-40 school year all Galloway children were bused to the new school, including my two sisters and me. We rode buses owned, and sometimes also operated, by persons such as Port Smith, Jess Clark, Louis Phillips, and Carl Daniels. Most were or once had been been Galloway residents. We waited for the bus each morning in small "bus shanties" located near each child's home. These were fairly effective in protecting us from rain, icy wind and snow. The bus rides usually were free from excess noise or student misbehavior, with proper behavior enforced by threat of being forced off the bus to walk the rest of the way. I recall this happening only a couple of times.

Students first entering the school in most of the years from 1939 until the late1950s attended classes in the same building for all their grades. Around 1960 a new elementary school was built in another section of the village of Rocky Grove, and students attended there until transferring to the 1939 school for their remaining school years.

During our elementary grades 1st through 6th all our teachers were female. Discipline was strict, and classrooms generally organized and quiet at least into the 1950s when I no longer attended school. Acceptable behavior in elementary school sometimes was enforced by physical means, including slaps to the face or paddling of misbehaving students. I remember only a couple of slapping incidents. A rumor once spread among classmates that the principal had an "electric paddle" which he would use if a standard paddling proved insufficient to create desired behavior modification. Parents apparently supported such disciplinary measures by teachers, as they were not unlike those commonly used at home. Related to this I recall that many of my Galloway playmates adhered strictly to times they were to quit playing and return home, stating they would face a "lickin" with a switch or razor strap if they failed to do so.

I remember only one incident where an elementary age school child, or child of any age, struck back and hit a teacher. He was removed from the room by the male principal and taken home. Into the 1940s threats of corporal punishment extended to junior and even senior high school age for both boys and girls. It supposedly would be carried out by a muscular physical education teacher. (Today, of course, if such occurred it likely would lead to charges of assault and battery, or retaliatory violence by the student or his/her parents.)

Despite, or perhaps partially because of, the disciplinary methods, classroom decorum usually prevailed during elementary and junior high school. The latter then included grades 7 through 9. Each school day started with a pledge of allegiance to the American flag, and reading by the teacher of a passage from the Bible. Never mind that many of us did not truly understand the meaning of many of the words read; at least it was a ritual which brought organization to the morning. There were short recesses for going to the bathrooms, and there was an approximately hour long lunch period during which "bus students" ate food they had brought in their lunch boxes, or "pails" as some called them, and "town" students could walk or run home for lunch. In some cases home was up to a quarter mile away, so lunch had to be very quick. With all that exercise, it is not surprising that there were very few overweight classmates! I assume that on snowy days town students also brought a packed lunch box. And, I'm quite sure that on their ways home for lunch some students stopped for a Hershey, Baby Ruth" or Clark candy bar or bottle of "pop" at one of the several grocery stores near the school such as Wygants, Flickners or the Red and White store. All of those were at the corner of Parker Avenue and Fox Street in Rocky Grove.

During lunch period, weather permitting, there usually was some time for being on the playground behind the school. High school students often ate lunch on the hillside below the Franklin Cemetery or played softball on the level areas, while younger ones played "kick ball". Occasional fights occurred primarily between elementary or junior high students. This would lead to calls of "fight, fight" by others who would rush in to see the action. Inevitably the fight soon would be halted by a teacher or school custodian who would hurry to the scene. Some playground bullying occurred as well. I recall one especially feared fifth grade boy who seemed to delight in "beating up" others just for the fun of it. One day I threw a hard-packed snowball quite a distance, accidentally hitting him in the face. I can still clearly recall seeing it hit his cheek, leaving a round white spot. Apparently no one saw me throw it, and I was not about to volunteer a confession as he angrily roamed around the playground trying to find the person who had dared hit him. Another time during eighth grade a somewhat older and bigger boy who seemed to enjoy picking on quite non-athletic me pushed me one too many times and I pushed back. By chance, he was standing on a patch of ice, and the push knocked him flat on his behind. I recall his look of disbelief as he stood up and regained his composure. I guess he felt he had misjudged my strength, because there was no further bullying.

Our teachers were motivated to provide us with good educational experiences, and in this I believe they succeeded quite well. I have many memories of the school days. For example, I recall that during early grades we had separate classes in penmanship during which we used metal-tipped pens which we dipped into in-desk glass "ink wells". During first grade much of our writing class consisted of drills to master neat production of series of "push-pulls" and "ovals". Perhaps because I was left- handed, or was male and hence more immature in visual-motor skills than girls at that age, I had much difficulty with this. I envied the productions of female classmates such as Mona Lou Pierce and Carol Nellis. At a reunion many years later I told Carol how I had been impressed with her "ovals" in first grade. She laughingly replied, "Are you sure that wasn't in eighth grade?"

Another early elementary school memory is that during the early years of this period special programs often were presented by a local chapter of the Women's Christian Temperance Union (WCTU). Since it had been only a few years after the 1933 repeal of prohibition of sales of alcohol, there may have been a perceived excessive use of "demon rum" by locals, and a felt need to educate children at an early age regarding the "evils" of alcohol use. Perhaps it was the passion with which these presentations were made that contributed to their being especially memorable.

There are many memories of elementary school teachers relating what they had learned during summer vacation travels, or during in -service educational experiences at Chautauqua Lake, N. Y. One especially memorable experience was my 5th grade teacher, Ms. Velma Heckerd, reading to us, in serial fashion, portions of children's stories such as Rikki Tikki Tavi. This, however, was provided we had been especially well-behaved that day. Such positive reinforcement may have been as effective as fear of her paddle!

Class instruction during elementary school usually was separate for so-called "A" class and "B" class students. Since IQ tests were not administered until later grades, this separation presumably was based on quality of a student's earlier school achievement. During this time period there was no classification of students as having "attention deficit disorder". In retrospect I believe there were very few, if any, in classes I attended who would have met today's definition of that disorder. Of course there were some who were much slower learners than others, but it was not until the mid-1960s that the term "learning disabled" became commonly used, and special education classes provided by school districts. And, it was not until the 1970s that students with major learning problems, then referred to as mentally deficient or retarded, were labeled and provided special public school education.

During my Rocky Grove High School (RGHS) days in the late 1940s and very early1950s, teaching quality remained high, and classroom discipline generally maintained. However, there were glaring exceptions, as when there was a substitute teacher or an overly permissive teacher. Then, loud talking among students, and passing of notes occurred to the degree that those of us who wished to learn found it difficult to concentrate. I recall this being especially true in a science class. But, there was one teacher of special note in regard to classroom discipline. That was our algebra teacher, Ms. Edith Heckerd, where discipline consistently was strict. Although probably no more than five feet, three inches tall, even the biggest boys respected and seemed to fear her. Perhaps it partially was because of the "withering" look she could give when she felt a student was out of line!

Two other high school memories stand out. It may have been in junior high, but there was this exciting day when someone called out, "helicopter", and we all rushed to the window to get our first glimpse of that type aircraft which we had only read about, or perhaps seen in movie newsreels. And, most of us long remembered the day our English teacher, Mrs. Deiter, brought a borrowed tape (or wire) recorder to class, and allowed each of us to hear his or her own recorded voice for the first time.

Of course there were no "drug problems" in local schools during these days. Terms commonly used in later years for marijuana such as "weed", "pot" and "grass" had different meanings for us: weed was something to remove from gardens, a pot usually was used for cooking and grass referred to the immaculate lawn surrounding the front of the school on which our principal forbade us to walk. The legal age for buying alcohol was twenty- one, and, to my knowledge, there was very little use by local high school boys and girls of that period. Similarly, despite the great many radio and magazine advertisements for cigarettes such as Lucky Strike, Kools, Old

Gold and Camels, few students smoked, and certainly never on school grounds. The rare girl who smoked was apt to be ostracized, and suspected of other types of "immorality".

By the late 1950s much was beginning to change especially in regard to cigarette use. But, it was not until the early to mid-1960s that many area residents became aware of use of illegal drugs by local persons of high school or college age. I believe the first time such became common knowledge was when several teenagers were arrested by undercover drug agents for possession of marijuana in the Franklin City Park. This is not to say that all local teenagers and young adults of the 1950s and earlier would not have tried illegal consciousness altering substances had they been readily available. I recall several friends of the time hinting that we could experience such effects by mixing aspirin and coca cola. It didn't work for us.

Throughout this period there was no strong local emphasis on higher education, i. e., college. I know of only six or seven other Galloway residents who went on to attain college degrees, and two of those were my sisters. However, it is very possible there were others especially after the early1950s of whom I never became aware. I'm sure this was due to lack of interest rather than to lack of academic aptitude. During those times there generally was full employment, with union pay scales commonly exceeding the salary of teachers, and of many other professions requiring a college degree. Even though tuition at state colleges such as Clarion was only approximately $70 per semester in the early 1950s, additional expenses as for dormitory and books made sending their children to college financially difficult for most Galloway families. Added to this was the fact that job opportunities for girls and women were much more limited than would become true during later decades. Thus, there was little incentive for higher education, and most persons my age opted to go to work in local factories immediately after high school, or after a few years of military service. Most were married by their early twenties.

Religion

As noted earlier there have been at least three different churches at Galloway over the years. However, during the period being covered here there was only the Galloway Methodist-Episcopal Church. Originally it was located at the top of the hill on the left hand side of Route 417, but has been on Seysler Road since1961. This church always has played a very important role in the spiritual and social lives of many Galloway residents. Especially during this 1937-1965 period residents such as Ruth Jacoby and Lucy Keith were instrumental in facilitating its growth and influence.

Original Galloway Methodist Episcopal Church (1930s)

My family had minimal contact with the Galloway Church. I do recall, however, welcome visitations to our home from church representatives at the time of my dad's passing. My sisters often attended Sunday school and church services at Franklin Methodist churches; and family weddings and funerals were Christian-oriented. I know that my mother believed in the power of prayer. I frequently attended church services while in the Army, but my personal religious orientation was based largely on my maternal grandmother's Christian Science teachings.

While on the topic of religion it may be of interest to some readers that for a time during the late 1940s Kathryn Kuhlman, a charismatic traveling evangelist, held healing services in tabernacles at Franklin and the village of Sugar Creek. She drew very large crowds there and later in Pittsburgh. I knew of Galloway residents claiming to have been cured of physical problems, one of whom was observed to walk without the crutches he had used for a long time. She later became nationally famous for her healing sessions and best selling books such as I Believe in Miracles.

Morals and Such

In this section I summarize my personal perceptions of matters such as stealing, lying, cussing, jealousies, prejudices and courting behaviors at Galloway and nearby regions during this period.

As previously mentioned regarding pre-1937 stealing of chickens, and my grandfather's experiences with attempted horse and payroll theft, some such crime did occur at Galloway. However, for most of the period covered here residents generally left home and car doors unlocked and had no regrets for it. Home invasions were nearly unheard of, and burglar alarm systems were non-existent or very rare. I do recall, however, an incident during the late 1930s where my grandparents experienced theft from their cellar of some of my grandmother's canned fruits. This prompted my grandfather and uncle Jim Rogers to rig an alarm system on the cellar door. Thereafter, grandfather kept his Harrington and Richardson revolver beside his bed. Shooting a horse thief during the earlier days of the 20th century likely would have been considered legally justified, but a jelly thief, maybe not!

As for lying and cussing by children, this sometimes was dealt with by corporal punishment. Having one's mouth washed out with soap which some parent's practiced might also qualify as such. Whether due to such suppression methods in childhood, religious teachings or parental modeling of "proper" behaviors, my experiences were that most Galloway adults spoke honestly, and cussed very little compared to present standards. For example, many business deals were "sealed" with a handshake, and many local grocers trusted residents to pay their accumulated bills each month. Cussing was common, especially among some men, but usually not in the presence of women or children. Commonly used swear words were "s-o-b", "b_ _ _ _ _d", "G_ d d_ _m", along with bathroom (or out-house)-related words. At least through the 1950s the "F-word" was rarely used by local men. And, if used by a girl or woman it almost surely would have marked her as promiscuous. I recall one instance which I thought mildly hypocritical where a Galloway girl used a much less extreme swear word in front of her mother, who then angrily said, "Stop that. It sounds like hell to hear a girl swear!"

Jealousies and prejudices existed of course, but often in different contexts from those commonly of concern during later years, or in other parts of the world. At least that is how I perceived it. There were vast differences in wealth between all, or nearly all, residents of Galloway during this period and that of, for example, persons living in the Miller Park region of Franklin.

However, I remember very few persons expressing resentment or jealousy concerning the disparity. More often the attitude seemed to be that those people either had invested wisely, or inherited their money from wealthy ancestors who had sold land during the oil boom. And, in any event, most were their employers, and/or had been responsible for bringing industry and jobs to the region. As for prejudice, it is to be remembered that nearly all Galloway residents of that time were what sociologists often referred to as WASPS, that is, white, anglo-saxon protestants. Nearly all were descendants of early settlers from the British Isles or northern Europe. There were no African-American or Oriental families at Galloway, and very few in Franklin. To my knowledge, the Spezialy family with ancestral roots in Italy was the sole exception during this period. They were an honest, very hard-working family and active in Galloway village affairs. Those may be reasons I never observed any prejudicial attitudes toward them. Racial prejudice was not an issue at Galloway during this period.

I do recall, however, my mother telling of local prejudice and hostility toward some immigrants from southern Europe during earlier times, the 1920s I believe. She recalled resentment that some such persons were moving to the region and willing to work for lower wages, thus costing jobs for local persons. And, some were perceived to be getting rich by illegally making and selling liquor ("hooch") during prohibition years. Apparently at places within the county there were some Klan marches associated with such resentment. She also recalled that, although they wore hoods, marchers' statures sometimes gave away their identity, causing much embarrassment for some of their family and friends.

Courting-Related Behavior

Sexual matters rarely were openly discussed during these years, especially prior to the 1960s. I suspect that few Galloway parents had "the talk" in any except the most basic details. Many of us likely first learned about the "birds and bees" from observing mating behaviors of animals. Some young children tried to satisfy curiosity regarding anatomical differences by quite innocently "playing doctor" with each other, Such activity today might lead to legal charges of sexual misconduct.

Of course, with the hormones of adolescence sexual matters usually took "center stage". It was fairly common for some boys to pass around sexually oriented notes in classes, and for "off-color"(aka "dirty") jokes to be whispered among students. Such were usually accompanied by lascivious facial expressions by the boys, looks of embarrassment from the girls and stern warnings from teachers if they discovered the activity. By the late 1950s some high schools, including Rocky Grove, were offering sex education lessons in "health" classes. Ours were taught by the boys' and the girls' physical education teachers, separately of course. Basic male-female anatomical differences were taught, but not much more. I don't recall any mention of topics such as homosexuality or masturbation, even though at the time there still remained a belief among some that the former was a type of psychiatric disorder, and the latter could lead to all manner of physical disorder. For many years most of us recalled the day our teacher, coach Vince Curran, forgot to erase his blackboard illustrations of male anatomy after class, eliciting many giggles from the girls in the next class to enter that room.

After high school opportunity for single persons to meet potential marriage partners was limited. During this time which was decades before personal computers, the internet and dating sites couples often met at church or social gatherings such as square dances. Some were introduced by friends or relatives who "fixed them up" with a date. Especially if she did not know him well, few girls or women would be "forward" enough to approach a male to initiate a date. This seems to have been due more to believing it would be "improper" than to fear of harm. It was not unusual for a young man to approach a female, introduce himself and attempt to arrange a date. I recall twice during my early twenties approaching an unknown, but attractive-looking girl, introducing myself and asking her to accompany me to a movie that weekend. In both cases she accepted, and soon we were dating

By high school and young adulthood the dates of boys and men who had cars often included "parking" in lover's lanes or a drive-in theater at night, and engaging in amorous activities with their girlfriend. At Galloway such sites often were on isolated oil lease roads where couples were unlikely to be disturbed, or caught. The scent of perfume blending with that of crude oil from nearby wells likely was long-remembered by many participants. These amorous activities sometimes were referred to as "necking" by persons of my older sister's age, and later as "petting" or "making out". At the time it was common for boys and young men to use baseball analogies when reporting on their parking experiences. For example "getting to first base" usually meant their activity involved no more than hugging and kissing, while "second" and "third base" referred to activities some politely labeled "heavy petting". A "home run", of course, meant "going all the way". Males generally were prone to exaggerate, and tried to give the impression that they were "Babe Ruths of the back seat". Girls, on the other hand, if they engaged in such talk at all, were prone to imply that they either did not play ball or stayed on first base. I do recall, however, that at many of these lease road sites one could find latex evidence that some "home runs" had been scored!

During this period it was very common for girls to remain virgins until marriage. If an unwed girl became pregnant it was expected she would drop out of school at least by the time her pregnancy was visibly obvious. Paternity testing was not available, and it was expected that the purported father of the child would marry her. I do not recall any literal "shot-gun weddings" at Galloway, although some may have occurred. There were very few sexually promiscuous girls in the area, and they nearly always were socially shunned by other girls, and rejected by boys as potential marriage partners. In later years it might have been suspected that such girls had been victims of sexual abuse; but males of the time, if they thought about it all, were likely to believe that they simply had naturally high hormone levels.

Local boys and young men were well aware of the term "jail bait". Nevertheless, dating of fifteen, sixteen or seventeen year old girls by slightly older males was not uncommon. Legal charges of statuary rape, or any type rape for that matter, were rare. And, it was my impression that, had it occurred, the accused offender was more likely to be "punished", or the situation otherwise "handled", by the girl's brother(s) or other family members than by police.

Various developments during the 1950s set the stage for the sex revolution of the early 1960s following which much of the above description of local sexual behavior no longer would apply. Such developments often are reported to have included publication of Hugh Hefner's Playboy Magazine, publication of Alfred Kinsey's reports on Sexual Behavior in the Human Male and Female, and, of course, sales of "the pill" beginning in 1959. Elvis and rock and roll music also were implicated by some. I recall a night about 1956 when a friend and I had dates with two sisters from a village near Galloway. While waiting for them in the living room of their home we heard the song Blue Suede Shoes being played in an adjoining room, and observed our dates' younger sister dancing to it. Her mother then charged into the room yelling "You turn off that evil music now!" By 1965 such would have seemed laughable to most. But it would remain for future generations to learn about and consider formerly unheard of, or strictly taboo topics such as pedophilia, incest, bi-sexuality, and sexual abuse and harassment.

Despite what some might consider limited or otherwise poor preparation for courtship and marriage, there were very few divorces among Galloway families during this period.

Medical and Dental Care

During this entire period it was common for local physicians to make house calls. Most were what today would be referred to as general practitioners. However, a few were known to have specialized training, interests or talents, and usually were the ones who performed the more complex operations at the local hospital. I recall my grandparents and parents mentioning names such as Dr. Rose Dunn, Dr. Zerby, and Dr. Foster, who apparently were prominent local physicians early in the 20th century. But, by 1937 other names are more memorable; for example, Drs. Phillips, Cunningham, Blanchard, Beals, Butters, Nordstrom, and McCandless. Dr. Nordstrom was an "eye/ear/nose/throat" physician, perhaps not as specialized as would be considered necessary to qualify as a specialist today but more so than most of the others.

I was considered a rather "sickly" child prior to about age ten, actually being absent from school nearly half of my second grade year with usual childhood diseases such as measles, chicken pox and mumps. Additionally, I once experienced what Dr, Phillips thought may have been rheumatic fever. It resulted in a permanent heart murmur, and doctor's orders to refrain from strenuous physical activities. I understand that it had been so severe that he once questioned if I would live through the night. However, he sent to Pittsburgh for a dose of what I believe was a sulfa drug, and I rallied within a few hours of receiving it. I was told that Dr. Phillips had stayed by the bedside for hours, and upon the breaking of my fever, told my very worried mother, "Well, that drug did it again!". Another memorable "family doctor" event occurred when my younger sister, Judy, experienced a severe nose bleed which our mother could not control. She made a frantic phone call to Dr. Blanchard who immediately raced from Franklin to Galloway. We lived at Colonia at the time, and there was deep snow surrounding the house. He missed our driveway, but turned into Infield Drive, stopped at the Ernest Frankenberger home, jumped out of his car, medical bag in hand, and rushed the last sixty yards to our back door. He arrived in time to stop the bleeding, perhaps saving my sister's life.

Such events emphasize advantages of the personal doctor-patient relationships of times gone by. However, Galloway area medical services during the 1937-1965 period sometimes left much to be desired. Many residents rarely or never were admitted to a hospital. This was before Medicare and medical health insurance as we know it today, and many residents may not have been able to afford hospitalization. Others apparently believed it was safer to stay at home than be hospitalized. There were stories of family members or neighbors who had gone for supposedly minor operations and died during a surgical procedure. For example, I recall a story that one of my mother's best friends went for what her family believed was simple removal of a small growth on her neck and died during the operation. A frequently repeated family story was of an aunt who died in a local hospital during the 1920s when a doctor apparently mistook a tumor for pregnancy. Of course, medical errors were not necessarily more frequent in that region than elsewhere. They may, however, have contributed to the attitudes I often heard expressed about dangers of hospitalization.

During those days a cancer diagnosis very often was equivalent to a death sentence. And, recovery from a heart attack was less common than today. In part this may have been due to early warning signs being unknown or ignored, or to hesitancy to be hospitalized until a disease had reached advanced stages. But, it also is likely that many smaller hospitals simply did not have sufficient specialized knowledge or needed surgical and other facilities to deal with some diseases. I believe most residents would agree that by the mid to late 1960s hospital services improved significantly when arrangements were made to team with Pittsburgh hospitals and medical schools and have more specialized physicians practice part-time at local hospitals.

By this period tuberculosis no longer was the major health concern in the region it had been a few years earlier. Nevertheless, as elementary school children we were tested for it. Polio, however, was a major concern until the Salk vaccine became available in the very early 1960s. There were occasional local outbreaks which often prompted quarantines. I recall one Rocky Grove school student dying and others being disfigured from it.

During all except about the last five years of this period local mental health treatment was non-existent. Persons suffering from major mental disorders such as schizophrenia or depression were sent to the large state hospital at North Warren, PA, approximately seventy miles from Galloway. Once there, it often became their permanent residence since there was little or no effective treatment provided in such facilities. During much of this period electroshock and prefrontal lobotomy were considered treatments of choice, both of which had major side effects such as loss of memory, brain damage-induced lack of impulse control, and impairment in ability to sustain attention. It was not until the discovery of what came to be known as anti-psychotic, anti-depressant and tranquilizing drugs in the late 1950s and early 1960s that this situation changed. Around that time mental health services came to nearby Oil City when a county mental health center opened. It was administered by a social worker named Richard Loring, and staffed with one or two part-time psychiatrists from North Warren. I also worked there part-time as a psychologist during the 1963-1965 period. A few years later, Dr. Carol (Nellis) Maurer, a fellow RGHS graduate, was employed there full time as a psychiatrist; yes, the same Carol whose "ovals" I admired in our first grade handwriting classes. Residents of Galloway and other regions of the county finally could receive psychotherapy and/or medication for a wide range of emotional, behavioral and mental disorders.

I don't recall names of the local dentists I consulted during this period. I do remember that many older Galloway residents had false teeth. Perhaps this was because our water had no fluoride, because many had diets conducive to tooth decay, and/or because trips to the dentist were expensive and painful. Whatever the reasons, it was common for some middle aged and older residents to travel to the Sexton Clinic in Florence, S. C. where teeth could be extracted and dentures prepared and fitted within a day or two at very low cost. I recall cases where members of two or more local families made the trip, sometimes considering it a vacation of sorts.

I can attest to some dental procedures being painful back then. Many times I sat in a dentist's chair in an office overlooking Liberty Street in Franklin, and felt sharp pain as his drill buzzed, or he squeezed a bulb to pump hot air onto a sensitive tooth. The latter apparently was done to dry it prior to filling a cavity. I suspect that one or more local dentists I consulted unnecessarily extracted some teeth. That was suggested by the comments, "Why are you missing so many teeth? What kind of dentist did you go to?" made by a dentist I consulted shortly after moving from the area. With the advances in dentistry which have occurred, I imagine that dentists of the region now are attentive to client comfort and attempt to save teeth when possible.

Food, Drink and Language

In this section I mention briefly some of what I recall having been frequent, or unique, items in the diets of Galloway residents of his period, as well as some unique choices of words. Of course these were not true for all residents, or restricted to Galloway. Many were characteristic of much wider regions in those times (and now), perhaps especially in rural parts of what generally is referred to as Appalachia.

Because it was common in this period for children to be invited to eat lunch, or "supper" as most called the late afternoon meal, I had opportunities to sample the menus of several families. Thus, the following is not based solely on the menus of my own family.

Even during the earlier years of this 1937-1965 period very few families had a cow, or cows, to supply milk as had been true earlier in the century. Most milk was supplied through dairies, such as Judson's in Franklin, and was purchased at local grocery stores or delivered by a "milkman". Many homes did have small gardens and orchards supplying tomatoes, potatoes, onions, beans, corn, lettuce and other vegetables and fruits in season. And, especially early on, a few kept chickens for a supply of eggs, and the occasional fried chicken meal. Many housewives "canned" fruits and vegetables to be eaten during off-seasons, often storing them in cupboards or potato bins in cool basements. However, after World War II, the vast majority of foods on the tables of Galloway families came from small grocery stores such as Stewart's or Flickner's stores in Rocky Grove, or the larger A &P store in Franklin. Eventually most was purchased from other larger stores nearby such as Krogers and Loblaws. Some Galloway residents took advantage of grocery delivery services which several smaller stores provided.

Breakfasts usually consisted of the usual bacon (or sausage) and eggs and/or pancakes. At Galloway and surrounding areas the latter often were made with buckwheat flour and a small cake of yeast with the "batch" having been prepared the night before. That allowed for fermentation and, hence, improved flavor. Some sprinkled sugar on their morning "buckwheat cakes", while others used maple syrup if available and affordable. Children often ate hot cereals such as Ralston whose producer provided child-oriented radio advertisements regarding how western ranch children such as "Jane and Jimmy" say, "Ralston cereal can't be beat". Of course there were many other breakfast foods to pick from. I recall that my grandfather's choice was shredded wheat with a sliced banana on it. After WWII many boxed cereals became available, including Wheaties, "The Breakfast of Champions" as it was advertised. A fruit juice such as orange or grape usually went along with breakfast, and, just as today, adults usually had coffee. However, during much of this period many local families would not permit children to drink coffee or tea at any time. As I recall, there were fears that such drinks could stunt one's growth.

I don't remember much about home lunches, but suspect that for most they consisted of the same foods our mothers commonly placed in our school lunch boxes and our father's work lunch pails. That would have been peanut butter and banana, or ham and cheese sandwiches, often with an apple included. A pint- sized thermos of cold milk for children, and hot coffee for the men would be included.

Supper menus basically were the same as commonly seen today: meat such as hamburgers, hot dogs, pork chops, chicken, or occasional steak when it could be afforded, green beans, and baked potatoes. The latter usually were with skin on, and mashed with one's fork prior to buttering, salting and peppering. Apple pie was a common dessert, and milk, water or hot tea were the usual drinks. Special treats were breads or rolls spread with home-canned preserves such as blackberry, raspberry, strawberry or elderberry jam or jelly, or buckwheat honey. Of course, in later years many of the preserves and other treats were "store bought" as many older Galloway residents labeled them.

During the earlier years of this period if a Galloway resident wanted to "eat out", and could afford to do so, there were Riddle's restaurant and the L & C restaurant on Liberty Street in Franklin. The latter also was a frequent meeting place for high school and college age persons for much of this period. And, a few stores further down on Liberty was Isalys where great sandwiches, as well as ice cream sundaes, sodas with real fruit, and ice cream cones in a great many flavors were sold. One flavor was labeled "rainbow", a blend of flavors with several different colors. "Double barrel" type cones could be purchased which accommodated two scoops side by side. The scoops of ice cream could be had in an elongated spear-like configuration as well as the usual rounded shape.

By the 1950s there were several additional eating places near Galloway, including at least two drive-in or drive up types. The former included Schenck's in Reno. One could eat-in or have an order taken by a waitress who would come to the car. I don't recall any being on roller skates as often seen in movies from the fifties. A unique feature, however, was that if one had a car radio it could be tuned to a certain wavelength and occupants could hear any music which might be playing on the restaurant's juke box. I believe that, almost undoubtedly, the drive-up most visited by Galloway residents back then and perhaps even now was located on Route 322 just past the Amoco oil refinery at the point where Patchel Run empties into French Creek. Originally many referred to it as "the tastee-freeze" due to its unique offering of the then new "soft" ice cream. Then for many years it was referred to as "Bears" which was the owner's last name. I don't recall exactly when, but at some point, perhaps not until the 1970s or later, it came to be known as "Pollys". Many local residents will recall sitting in their '57 Chevy ('62 Ford, etc) on warm summer evenings, enjoying their window purchases of hot dogs, sodas with real fruit such as black raspberries, and ice cream cones they had chosen from among the many different flavors being offered that day.

Some common soft drinks of the period are worth mentioning, especially some rarely or never heard of today. If one had opened a store's "pop" cooler in this period, coca cola, pepsi cola and royal crown cola would be choices just as today. Some would be in bottles of different shape, making them collectible antiques now. Other then-popular, but now infrequently seen flavors also would be in the cooler including birch beer, cream soda, lemon/lime and squirt. The latter was somewhat similar to today's 7-up. Many other bottles of different flavors such as orange and lime would be from the Nehi company.

Beer drinkers of the day would find plenty of Carlings Black Label, Rolling Rock and Schlitz in a cooler, along with some bearing Pittsburgh-related names such as Duquesne (pronounced "DuKane") and Iron City. I especially recall an early TV advertisement for the latter which depicted a group of burly steel workers leaving a mill at closing time and entering a tavern. One shouts "give me an iron", whereupon the bar tender in a macho manner forcefully shoves a bottle of Iron City beer down the bar to the thirsty steel worker. Young women of the period, if they drank beer, often preferred Miller High Life with its tapered long neck bottle. As for "hard" drinks it was common for young men on a date to coolly order "Jack and ginger on the rocks", and for his date to order a "sloe gin fizz".

As noted above, most Galloway language "differences" were not truly different from much of Appalachia. For example, although some families such as mine never used the word "ain't", it was common in rural areas such as Galloway and often used in popular country songs. Among Galloway residents, and throughout much of western Pennsylvania and West Virginia, small streams which elsewhere often are referred to as "brooks", were, and are, called "runs", while somewhat larger streams are labeled "creeks" but pronounced "cricks". Still larger streams, as elsewhere, are rivers. If a person around the Galloway region, referred, for example, to the village or stream of Sugarcreek as "Sugarcreek" and not "Sugarcrick" it would either mark him or her as an outsider, or a local who considered themselves "just a little better" than others. At Galloway as in much of Western Pennsylvania it was, and is, common to use the term "redd-up" as a synonym for clean-up or organize, as in "go redd-up your room".

Other terminology recalled which may have been more or less unique to Galloway, or at least to one or more of its residents, will be mentioned here. I remember one older man who often started a sentence with "me thinks". Perhaps this reflected his northern European or English ancestry. Others regularly would add "so I do" or "so he does" at the end of a statement, as with "He has the best rabbit hound I ever saw, so he does". I assume this was an attempt to accentuate the validity of the statement. Several neighbors pronounced "fish" as "feesh"; and hunting and fishing nearly always were pronounced without the ending g. Rather than saying "walking in the woods" some would say "out rammin the woods". My grandfather, as with many persons born in the 19th century frequently used the term "Oh-Pshaw", usually with a silent p. I believed at the time and still do that for him it was just a more socially appropriate version of "Oh-s_ _t". However, a recent dictionary defines it as "a way of expressing disbelief, contempt or irritation". During this period words such as "swell","neat", or by the 1960s, "groovy" often were used synonymously with today's "cool" which back then referred only to temperature. My sister's diary made many references to "swell" movies she had seen, books she had read, or new friends she had met.

Most of us referred to our mothers as "mum" rather than "mom", probably a reflection of our common English ancestry. For many of us a pumpkin was a "punkin", and a donkey was a "dunky". And, for unknown reason, some residents often used the adjective "old" (or more often, "ol") when mentioning another person regardless of actual age, as in, "Have you seen ol Bill lately?".

Recreational Activities

Many readers may wonder how Galloway residents of this period spent their leisure time. For many families life was much more work than play, especially during the earlier years, and especially for the adults. And, even most of my childhood friends had regular "chores" to do before they could play, such as weed gardens or "do the dishes" (wash, dry, put up). However, there was some "fun time".

During earlier portions of this period, before television, the radio played a large recreational role for all ages. By the late 1930s most Galloway families had at least one radio in the home, and, with proper aerials, could receive programs from at least a few stations such as KDKA Pittsburgh, and WSM, Nashville. I recall that at 7:00 PM my grandfather insisted on silence from wife and grandchildren so that he could focus on the nightly news as presented by Lowell Thomas. And, each weekday there was time set aside for my grandmother to listen to the soap opera-type program "Easy Aces". Saturday nights often were reserved for music of the Grand Ole Opry, which during the 1930s likely starred such performers as Jimmy Rogers. Other long-running radio favorites of families included The Inner Sanctum, Fibber McGee and Molly, and The Life of Riley. Gangbusters was one of my favorites, but was from WXYZ, Detroit, and the signal was very weak at our Galloway home. Many times, as an elementary school age child, I sat in my rocking chair with ear pressed to the radio speaker, attempting to separate signal from static in order to hear of the police activities and descriptions of wanted criminals. Other memorable favorites of children, and many adults, were Superman and the Lone Ranger with their dramatic introductions involving phrases such as "Look, up in the sky, its a bird, its a plane, no, its Superman", and "Return with us now to those thrilling days of yesteryear, the

Lone Ranger rides again". As the years passed many more stations and programs became widely available with game shows, soap operas, westerns such as Gene Autry "Riding the range once more", and many other genre. Many of these began to transition to TV by the middle 1940s.

By the late 1940s when many cars had radios, listening to Your Hit Parade became very popular among young people. Persons waited excitedly to discover what song would be #1 for the week; would it be Good Night Irene (circa 1949), or, "Tammy", or the hugely different "Jail House Rock" (1957)? One thing we knew for certain was that we would be hit with the program's cigarette advertisement: L.S.M.F.T. (Lucky Strike Means Fine Tobacco)! Incidentally, many of us at Galloway preferred the "Hillbilly Hit Parade" where the songs of performers such as Hank Williams, George Jones and Hank Snow were featured. As I recall, Hank Snow's Rhumba Boogie was # 1 for several weeks during my senior year of high school.

My first encounter with television was during the early 1940s when one afternoon my Dad and I happened to stop by a 13th Street store in Franklin, Vengold I believe. Several people were sitting around a table watching a rather "ghostly" and unstable picture of a face on the very small screen of a small box. We were told that it had been brought there to help determine how far from a Pittsburgh station this "television broadcast" could be received. Given the poor quality of the picture, I assume they decided that day that it was less than the eighty miles to Pittsburgh. But within three or four years that situation had improved greatly, and TV sets were advertised for sale by some local merchants. As noted earlier, the first set that I recall at Galloway was owned by the Schiffer family in the late 1940s. It created considerable excitement among the lucky friends and neighbors they invited to come and enjoy this new phenomenon with them. Throughout the remaining years of this period "watching TV" gradually replaced listening to the radio as a main source of entertainment as well as of information regarding state and world affairs. Although it was not always easy to enjoy consistently good reception, by strategically rotating their pole-mounted TV antenna Galloway viewers usually could access at least one Pittsburgh, Cleveland, or Erie station on their black and white sets. Many of their favorite radio shows and performers from earlier days were "on TV". Galloway residents, and sons and daughters of Appalachia everywhere, now could see and hear their favorite Grand Ole Opry stars as well as "newcomers" like Loretta Lynn and Johnny Cash, in live broadcasts from the Ryman auditorium in Nashville. During the 1950s and into the 1960s westerns also were especially popular. Saturday evenings were filled with offerings such as Bonanza, Gunsmoke and The Rifleman where clearly "good" guys for thirty minutes dealt Colt 45- or Winchester-enforced justice to unambiguously "bad" guys.

But, radio and TV had competition for Galloway residents' leisure time. The Orpheum and Park, and later the Kayton movie theaters on Liberty Street in Franklin were afternoon and evening destinations for many. For many years it was common to refer to movies as "picture shows" or just "shows". During earlier years of this period, for about twelve cents admission and another ten cents for popcorn, children could sit in either the balcony or downstairs of the Park and watch the latest episode of serial productions. I recall especially westerns such as Flaming Frontiers where we once waited anxiously for a week to see whether cowboy/scout Johnny Mack Brown had managed to elude hostile Indians surrounding a wagon train, and made it to a nearby fort to alert cavalry to come to their rescue. He did! And, for similar prices adults could attend the Orpheum for such classic 1939 movies as Stagecoach and Gone With The Wind. Some even were in the then-new "technicolor". For much of this era it was typical for there to be "news of the day", and a cartoon such as Woody Woodpecker, Bugs Bunny or Beaky Buzzard in addition to previews of coming attractions and the main feature film (or even two films in the case of "double features"). Many times a brief newsreel type film in documentary style also was included. An especially memorable series for me was The March of Time, narrated in dramatic fashion, and always concluding with the phrase, "And....time marches on". After the Park theater was destroyed by fire in the mid-1940s, the luxurious for the times Kayton was built at that location. For the remaining years of this period it became the local theater showing the more highly rated movies.

There was considerable violence portrayed in movies of those days, with fistfights and shootouts being common. However most were in black and white, and clearly identified villains "died" quickly with no apparent pain or loss of blood. The State Board of Censors saw to it that no sex scenes were shown. In fact, for some time even married couples were not shown in bed. This situation changed, though quite slowly, during the early 1960s.

While just a few years earlier nearby Monarch Park had been a favorite place for entertainment, by the late 1930s and for the remainder of this period Conneaut Lake Park about 40 miles northwest of Galloway became a favorite destination. Some famous bands were booked to perform; and local factories such as the "rolling mill" (Franklin Steel) often held company picnics there. I recall that loud music prevailed at the company picnics, with "Beer Barrel Polka" seeming to be a favorite. Many of us remember well the large "fun house" with its distorting mirrors and wide wooden sliding board, the many rides such as the whip and moon rocket, and spooky rides in the dark on the "pretzel" where demons and other scary creatures would suddenly appear around every other turn. And, few can forget the thrill of riding the "blue streak" if one dared. It was a wooden roller coaster which was "tame" by today's standards, but challenging enough that grown men could be observed daring each other to ride it. Some did so only after an alcohol- induced burst of courage. For young adults moonlight rides on the lake, and dancing as couples to the "big band sound" at the Pavilion or the "Cow Shed" were popular.

As very young children we Galloway kids used a lot of imagination playing with toy metal soldiers or cowboys, and often pretending to be one of them as we fought "enemies". By about the age of six I had multiple realistic- looking cap pistols which I used in a similar manner when I wasn't playing with my Marx electric train, listening to our radio, or playing tag or "red rover, red rover, throw the ball over" with neighborhood friends. Along with others of similar age and older I spent considerable time reading comic books such as Popeye and Dick Tracy. We could never have imagined that the first issue of the Superman comic costing no more than a dime would someday be worth thousands. By early teen age we often took toy guns to the woods where we pretended we were "commandos" (something like today's "special forces"). Often we tried to simulate war games where one group of three or four would go into the woods first and find a camouflaged hiding place to wait and "ambush" a second group which would be searching for us. If today's paint ball guns had been available back then there probably would have been less arguing over which side won.

Some young people of Galloway enjoyed roller skating at a Sugarcreek rink, and some teenagers and adults enjoyed bowling at a Franklin alley. For awhile during the 1950s some teenagers would join friends at the Rockette, a sandwich shop on Fox Street in Rocky Grove. There they could mingle, listen to favorite songs on the juke box, and perhaps dance. During our early teens several of us had bicycles which we could ride on the smoother lease roads, Infield Drive, and even Route 417 and Warren Road which had minimal traffic in those days. For some residents, adults included, a common past time was surreptitiously "listening in" on party line phone conversations. It was a great source of gossip. And, I recall my parents, apparently when bored, occasionally saying, "Let's go down town to Liberty Street and watch the people go by". At that time cars parked facing the sidewalk at a slight angle, permitting a clear view of store fronts and persons walking by on the sidewalk.

No account of Galloway recreation would be complete without mention of our very own country music venue, Hill

Billy Park, which existed for a few years in the 1950s. It was located in an open woodland and field section of the Burkhardt farm on the right hand side of 417 across the road from birch spring. In addition to local talent, some "big names" of country music of the time such as Little Jimmy Dickens performed there. On warm, sunny weekend afternoons sons and daughters of Appalachia from Galloway and other areas could enjoy a picnic lunch, or hot dogs from the small concession stand while their favorite country music reverberated through the nearby hills.

By teen-age most local boys followed in their fathers' and male relatives' footsteps to develop avid interests in fishing and/or hunting. Early spring saw many men sitting near small bonfires and fishing for suckers on the banks of such sites as the bend in French Creek just beyond the Fo Co refinery. And, because April 15th usually was the opening day of trout season, the banks of Two Mile Run, Sugar Creek, and many such streams were crowded at that time of year. Summer days brought out large numbers of fisherman seeking small mouth bass, walleyes or muskellunge on French Creek, the Allegheny River, Sugar Lake and other favorite fishing sites. I was an avid, but generally unsuccessful young fisherman. Most of my catches were colorful 6 to 9 inch brook trout caught at Patchel Run. An entry in a diary I kept around the age of eight read, "Today dad and mum took me up the crick to Port Smith's place. I caught four rock bass and a catfish. The catfish horned me and it hurt."

Most teen-age boys and men during this era owned or had access to guns for "plinking" tin cans, paper targets, etc., shooting clay pigeons, or hunting. I "graduated" from cap pistols, to a Daisy B-B gun, to a Marlin bolt action 22, to a rented 410 gauge, and finally to my own Stevens double barrel 16 gauge, and brand new 12 gauge Ithaca Model 37 pump shotgun. I was unable to afford a real "deer rifle" until the early1960s, so made do with rifled slugs in the Ithaca for deer hunting. That was not considered much of a sacrifice by older hunters who recalled that prior to invention of the more accurate and effective slugs, they used shells containing round balls of lead for hunting deer and bear with shotguns. Those shells went by names such as "punkin balls" or "bear balls" and were very inaccurate. As deer season approached each year I longed for a rifle such as Mr. Cheers' 32 Remington pump, or Mr. Jacoby's same model in 35 Remington, or Mr. Orr's 30-06 Model 70 Winchester.

Until at least the early 1960s, if a person wanted to buy a gun locally he or she would not find one of the large gun stores common today. Especially before the World War II years many guns were purchased through Sears and Roebuck catalogs. Most persons I knew bought theirs at local hardware stores such as Byer's Hardware in Franklin, or at sporting good stores such as the Army Store in Oil City, or the Varsity Sport Shop and Tom George's store on 13th Street in Franklin. The latter is especially memorable for me. Many times as a child of about nine to twelve I stood on the sidewalk looking into the store window at the various hunting and fishing-related goods on sale. Mr. George appeared reluctant to welcome such a young window shopper into the store. But, if I could talk my Father into taking me, I would make it in. It was a rather crowded small store which always smelled of tobacco and leather. For as long as possible, I would look at the various colorful fishing lures and pocket knives under counter glass, and stare at the wall behind the counter on the left side which held about twenty rifles and shotguns. These were from companies such as Winchester, Parker, Ithaca and A. H. Fox. There also were several shelves of ammunition, including even 8 gauge shotgun shells.

Hunting was one of the favorite past times of many Galloway men and boys. In addition to "game" animals which could be hunted only in season, there were no restrictions on hunting for crows, groundhogs, foxes or raptors such as hawks and owls. For many years the Pennsylvania Game Commission paid a bounty on foxes and raptors. That is in stark contrast to the years after 1972 when Federal law levied a several thousand dollar fine for killing or having in one's possession a hawk or owl.

Seasons for small "game" animals were only about four weeks long. The first day of small game season (primarily rabbits, grouse, squirrels, and, later, ringneck pheasants) was eagerly awaited, and often had been preceded by hours of "running the dogs". The latter involved taking one's dog or dogs, usually beagles, to woods and fields for training, getting them in shape for the coming season, or just listening to the "music" of dogs on the trail of game. Many of the Galloway "lease lands" with their fields of golden rod and sumac, large stands of crab apple trees and blackberry bushes, and occasional clumps of quaking aspen provided excellent cover for rabbits and grouse. Some years the grouse population was much higher than other years. I recall once during the mid 1940s flushing six or seven in one covey.

Despite ample game near home, many of us would drive elsewhere to hunt. This was true especially if hunting for pheasants which were more prevalent in adjoining counties such as Mercer and Crawford.

Although it may be difficult for today's hunters to believe, during this period very little land was posted with "no trespassing" signs. One could simply put guns and dogs in the car, drive to most any place which looked promising, and proceed to hunt. Nevertheless, we occasionally knocked on landowners' doors to ask permission, and it nearly always was granted. By the late 1950s this situation began to change slowly. I recall being surprised during the early 1960s when two different landowners in Crawford County angrily ordered me off their property. However, plenty of State Game Lands remained open which were well-stocked by the Game Commission. There never was much worry about having a place to hunt, or ever having to pay to hunt.

The first days of big game (deer/bear) season also were eagerly awaited. During the 1937-1965 period there essentially were no bears in Venango County, and there were few bear hunters from Galloway. It was the first day of deer season to which most hunters looked forward. It was about a two week "one-buck only" season. However, some years does could be taken during a later one or two day special season by hunters who had not taken a buck, and had their names drawn in a special lottery. Especially after WWII, opening day usually was the Monday after Thanksgiving. With the possible exception of Christmas eve, that day and the two preceding it saw more road traffic in towns such as Franklin than any other time of the year. Some towns offered very early morning buckwheat cake and sausage breakfasts; and long lines could be seen at stores selling ammunition.

I understand that there always were deer in the Galloway area. My mother told of occasionally seeing them grazing with cows in the open pastures of the early 20th century, but she did not recall any neighborhood men hunting them. During the early 1940s I recall seeing a few deer, but it seems it was not until after WW II that the local deer population grew quite fast and deer hunting became highly popular. Even so, for many years some Galloway hunters would go off on day trips or to hunting camps to hunt in what often was referred to as the "big woods" near towns such as Marienville, Ridgeway, and Owl's Nest. Deer there were so numerous that it was not unusual to see one hundred or more in a day. The vast majority, however, were does which legally could not be taken. By the late 1950s on the first day of deer season so many men and boys would "call in sick" or simply not show up for work or school that many local businesses and factories would close. I'm not sure of the date, but eventually opening day became essentially a state holiday with schools and businesses other than gun stores and restaurants closed. Stories and pictures of successful hunters and their trophies regularly appeared in the Franklin News Herald, and many persons would gather on main streets to view deer tied on car roofs and fenders. Deer-hunting readers may be interested to know that during most of this period very few hunters used scopes on their rifles, and nearly all hunted from ground stands rather tree stands. Some stalked deer, especially when there was tracking snow on the ground.

Before leaving this section it may be of interest to some that, despite broad interests in guns and hunting and despite watching gun violence in Western movies, there were very few gun-related crimes or accidental shootings at Galloway. Guns generally were viewed as something to be used for hunting or target shooting. Although rifles and shotguns often were displayed in plain sight in the corner of a room or in a glass-windowed and often unlocked gun cases, children knew and obeyed parental demands that they were not to be touched. Children usually were introduced to safe gun use by their fathers, starting with a B-B gun. By state law, a child could not legally hunt until age twelve, and then only in the company of a parent. At fourteen and fifteen one could hunt if accompanied by any adult family member, and by sixteen he or she could hunt alone. During this era police officers in many small towns went years without ever having need to draw their revolvers. My grandfather's above-mentioned taking his revolver to bed with him each night was an exception to this view of guns. Maybe because, as previously noted, he twice had been the victim of attempted robbery he was somewhat less trusting of people than usual for Galloway residents.

Perhaps because of televised news, by the mid to late 1950s there was some local talk of need for personal protection with a firearm. By the early 1960s I knew a few local men who were "carrying", and purchased a Ruger Single Six. Getting a permit was simple, requiring only a quick trip to the County Sheriff's Office where I had to show a driver's license. Upon telling the sheriff my Father's name, he immediately had his secretary type a permit for either open or concealed carry.

Even when walking down the streets of Franklin or Oil City with the pistol openly displayed, I was never questioned by law enforcement or anyone. Happily, I never had any need for the permit.

Participating in and/or following organized sports such as football, baseball and basketball was recreational for some Galloway residents. RGHS had no football team, and I don't recall any Galloway residents following NFL teams. I'm sure, however, that some were fans of the Franklin High School football teams during the late 1940s when Franklin's most famous athlete, Ted Marchibroda, was playing. He went on to play for St. Bonaventure College and the Pittsburgh Steelers, and coached several Baltimore teams for many years thereafter. An all-around athlete in high school, he also was named to the All-State High School Basketball team in 1949. I recall watching one Franklin High School basketball game, and marveling at his cat-like speed which made him stand-out from the other players as he repeatedly made steals.

As noted earlier, Galloway had its own baseball team for awhile during early years of the 20th century, but I could find no indications of a formal team thereafter. However, many residents followed the games of local teams such as existed for awhile in Rocky Grove, or were sponsored by companies such as the CPT. And, some were fans of the Cleveland Indians and/or Pittsburgh Pirates. I recall excitedly listening, along with the Orr family, to radio broadcasts of the 1948 World Series. The Indians, with players such as Larry Doby, one of the earliest African American players in the major leagues, defeated the Boston Braves. And, as this era was coming to a close I recall sitting in my 1956 Ford Victoria listening to the final game of the 1960 World Series when Bill Mazeroski's famous home run in the bottom of the ninth won the pennant for the underdog Pirates over the Yankees despite the latter having such famous players as Micky Mantle and Yogi Berra.

According to notices in the News Herald, for a few years during the 1940s Galloway actually had a basketball team known as the Galloway Bombers, with players such as Jim and "Junior" Frankenberger. However, for most of the years it was the RGHS Orioles basketball teams which were closely followed by a greater number of Galloway residents. Having been under doctor's orders to avoid strenuous exercise because of a heart murmur, and being rather "klutzy" as well, I never played basketball. But, from about seventh grade on I read about and admired the athletic skills of area stars. First it was Jack Biery of Franklin; and then in the 1945 and 1946 seasons it was Bruce Wagner of Cochranton High School who averaged 23 points per game. That led some local newspaper sports writers to make announcements such as, "Wagner and company will be playing..... (whatever team Cochranton High was to play)".

RGHS had some exceptional teams during these years, probably most notably the 1948-1949 season when they won the Class B district championship. That qualified the team for a trip to Bradford to play the Kane wolves in an inner-district playoff game. I recall making the trip to Kane in a chartered bus with a large number of RGHS students. We were much more excited on the trip up than on the trip back because the wolves defeated our orioles despite the best efforts of our cheerleaders and star players such as as Son

Buck, Corky Hunter, Bob McClimans and Carl Knoch (pronounced Knox).

I remember some of our team's cheers and "fight" songs. A silly, but rather creative one in junior high school was: "Big banana, little banana, we're from Gary, Indiana; that's a lie, that's a lie we're from Rocky Grove Junior High". Well, it was rhythmic and easily remembered. I believe that words to one of our songs included, "Oh, when the orange and black come down the floor, we know that they will always, always score". It was wishful thinking much of the time. During my senior year our team had some good nights, but, as I recall, more games were lost than won. Although News Herald accounts often described our players, such as Jack Adams, Bill Karns and Tom Gibbons, as "hard driving" or scrappy, when the tallest players on a basketball team are no more than 5 feet,10 inches tall success on the court can be "difficult".

As Judy (Jacoby) Lusher recently reminded me, one of the simple pleasures for many Galloway residents during the 1949-1978 period was to stop by our home to see and listen to my mother's parrot named Mac. "He" kept that name for years, even though at one point Mac laid an egg, and some suggested the name should be should be changed to "Maxine". Mac had several preferred phrases including, "Have a cup of tea", "Hit the trail", and, of course, "Polly want a cracker". These were enunciated quite clearly, often seemingly were used appropriately for a given situation, and sometimes learned very quickly. For example, there was the time I was very hurriedly doing something and my mother said "Where's the fire?". Almost immediately Mac began using that phrase.

Miscellaneous Galloway "Adventures"

In this section I describe some personal Galloway-related events which to me qualified as adventures at the time, and do so even now in memory. Realizing that one's personal memories are apt to be of little or no interest to many others, I limited these to stories which I believed would have general human interest, or special meaning for present and past Galloway area residents with interests in trout fishing, deer hunting, and/or early history of the Rocky Grove Volunteer Fire Department (RGVFD). In keeping with the book's title, most stories also provide some information on geography and customs of the Galloway of this era.

Explorations. I guess I always have been an explorer. My very earliest memory was of making a forbidden trip upstairs at the age of three to the third floor attic of the Rocky Grove Avenue home where I was born. My Mother soon found me surrounded by wasps, and crying because I had pricked a finger on one of the sharp nail-like parts of her curtain stretchers. Three years later we were living at Colonia, where a forbidden venture would be to travel the hundred yards or so to highway 417, cross it, and proceed further. Nevertheless, one afternoon I slipped away and did just that. Excitedly, but rather fearfully, I crossed the highway and walked about another hundred yards down a lease road to a deserted stretch where I sat alone in silence overlooking a barren spot among a stand of crab apple trees. I was feeling rather lonely and scared when a rabbit suddenly emerged from the surrounding goldenrod and hopped toward me. We stared at each other for a few minutes, perhaps somehow communicating. The rabbit then slowly hopped away, and I returned safely home. I never forgot that trip. To my six-year-old mind it must have been comparable to what some future astronaut will experience when exploring alone a distant planet, and a friendly alien steps out to greet him or her from behind a boulder of an otherwise barren surface.

Maybe the positive experience with that rabbit helped to counteract the earlier traumatic attic exploration. Once when telling this story to friends they reminded me that I have been an "attic" explorer most of my life, as a psychologist exploring the "attics" of clients: their minds and brains. Since many of those persons are convicted felons or seriously mentally ill persons, their "attics" sometimes hold content of even greater potential danger than wasps and the sharp edges of curtain stretchers!

If you Google the term "Patchel Run" you will see it described as a 3.41 mile stream in Pennsylvania "arising on the Wolf Run divide about two miles Northwest of Galloway, then flowing South to meet French Creek. Named after an early settler, Edward Patchell, it drains 6.76 square miles, with an average annual flow of 5.99 cubic feet per second. This rather sterile description is not nearly as rich as my perception of the stream or that of many other past and present residents of Galloway. As boy of eight or nine I had heard many stories of the Patchel Run valley, such as its having been the home of my maternal great grandparents, and multiple other families, the site of much oil excitement during the late 1800s and early

1900s, and the destination for picnics by many of the young people of Galloway.

I longed to visit there. Knowing its general location and being in explorer mode, I set off alone from Colonia one day hoping possibly to see the stream. I crossed 417 and headed West following lease roads to where level land ended and the land sloped down, sometimes quite steeply, for about a quarter mile. Probably fearing that my parents would note my absence and worry that I might be lost, I came close to turning back when three fourths of the way down. But then I heard the faint sound of running water, and proceeded another fifty yards or so where I was thrilled to actually see Patchel Run! After a strenuous uphill climb I returned home afraid for some time to tell anyone of my adventure. By age eleven I had talked my parents into buying for me a casting rod and reel, a creel, a belt-mounted worm box and hip boots. And for the next three or four years I made many more spring and early summer trips to the stream to try to fill the daily limit of ten native brook trout from the shallow, crystal clear water. I usually went alone. However, one year a beagle I nick-named "Bum" unexpectedly appeared and often would follow me and sit on the forested banks of the stream, keeping me company as I fished.

For the first couple of years my usual routine was to walk from home to the site where I initially had seen the stream, try my luck in the relatively deep (two to three feet), calm water at that location, then walk upstream on a path beside the run for about a hundred yards to where a smaller tributary entered. Then I would step into the main stream, letting my worm-baited hook drift downstream through riffles and into slower moving "holes" as I waded back to the original location. It was common to catch a half dozen or more trout of six to nine inch size, which I then would take home for my mother to cook.

During following years I sometimes fished with a friend, often Henry Jacoby, and we expanded our range. We labeled the tributary mentioned above as "Litte Patchel Run" and traced its origin to birch spring. It also contained many trout, especially around the site of remnants of an old water wheel which once had been used as a source of power for pumping nearby oil wells. We referred to the main Patchel Run stream above the mouth of "Little Patchel" as White Run because we had been told that its origin was a spring house on the White Farm near Keely Corners. That portion of the Run also held many trout.

I never caught a trout larger than nine inches in length at the Run. However, I recall that once a few yards downstream from the point where I had first viewed the stream I came across what may have been its only truly deep hole. The bottom could not be seen at that shady location. When I let my worm drift into it there was a strike which bent my rod, nearly knocking it out of my hand. But, "the big one always gets away", and that one did. I fished that hole several times later, to no avail. I know though that something larger than nine inches lurked there. Several years later as a sixteen year old hiking along the lower portion of what Henry and I had called White Run, I carefully crept on hands and knees to a bank overlooking a clear, slow moving pool. There, to my great surprise, were two large trout, at least fourteen to sixteen inches in length. I reported what I had seen to Henry, who did not seem especially surprised. He told me that his uncle and grandfather, while fly fishing near the old water wheel had caught some twelve inch size trout on Little Patchel. Perhaps by that time I was more interested in hunting and other pursuits than in fishing, and was content with memories of my exciting earlier childhood explorations of Patchel Run. For whatever reasons I never fished the Run again.

Visiting the River Ridge Farm. Many of today's children experience the adventures of visiting castles and famous landmarks around the world, if not in person with parents or grandparents, then by realistic virtual visits via their computers or cell phones. However, except for some movie experiences, only a child of a wealthy family could do so in the 1937-1965 period. Nevertheless, some of us did get to experience the adventure of visiting our own local "castle": the thirty-three room Sibley mansion on the River Ridge Farm overlooking the Allegheny River between Franklin and Oil City. Because our Father cared for the owner's dogs during much of this period, my sisters and I occasionally would accompany him on his house (or mansion) calls there. To us, those trips were as much, or more, of an adventure than if we were visiting the Taj Mahal. I recall there being two roads leading to the farm, one of which had a small stretch where there was a precipitous drop off on the Allegheny River side. My sister Judy always covered her eyes or sat on the car floor as we passed that area. On either route it was required that we stop at a large gate house to be approved for entry. Upon arriving at the mansion we were greeted by servants who took us children to a very large basement room and gave us milk, cookies and cake, while dad attended to the owner's dogs.

Occasionally we went to the first floor and were allowed to sit in the huge living room with a great view of the Allegheny River Valley, and the remaining buildings of the Eclipse Oil Works. I had seen and used binoculars, but nothing like the powerful ones the servant allowed me to use to better appreciate the view. She referred to those as "field glasses". I recall there being large gardens surrounding much of the mansion, and several large, very shiny cars, probably Packards or Cadillacs, in the drive with chauffeurs standing by. The entire scene was such a great contrast to what we were used to. In retrospect, I'm surprised they let us in with our Ford rather than sending a chauffeur to bring us! In fact, on one occasion they did just that. The owner had purchased a German shepherd from a Cleveland, Ohio owner, and wanted Dad to pick it up. I was allowed to ride along, and sat in the back seat with the dog on the way home. The one thing I remember most about the trip was the size of the car, especially the long distance between the front of the back seat and the back of the front seat. It seemed to me that if I had a ball, the dog and I could have played throw and retrieve back there.

There are many written accounts of the history of River Ridge Farm. Very briefly, the mansion was built in 1913 by Joseph Sibley who had become a multi-millionaire largely through his co-ownership of the Galena Oil Works in Franklin. He developed an oil product which enabled greatly improved and safer lighting for trains, as well as an excellent lubricant for railroad signals. The products sold very well world-wide, and the company later was purchased by Standard Oil. Mr. Sibley died in 1926. It was surviving members of his family who owned and operated the farm during the years my father consulted with them.

Surviving a Galloway Winter. If one has never lived through a winter in a cold northern climate such as that of Galloway, he or she probably would not understand how the coming of spring might be considered an adventure. During most of the period covered here, winter snowfall often was heavy and stayed on the ground for weeks or months at a time. Main roads often were covered with snow and ice or were very muddy, making it treacherous to travel. And smaller ones such as the lease roads often were impassable for periods of time. Temperatures often dropped far below zero, with daily highs well below freezing. Diseases such as flu, pneumonia, and common childhood diseases were more prevalent during the winter months. There were no snowmobiles or nearby ski resorts for recreation, golf courses were closed, and after December 15th both fishing and hunting seasons were over. Children generally adapted well, with sled riding, snowball fights, building of "snow forts", etc. But, many adults, especially senior citizens, felt restricted and isolated, and longed for signs of spring. Thus, it should not be surprising that for many Galloway residents certain rituals took place from late January through March involving preparation for spring. Much excitement was felt about signs that it was imminent, or actually had arrived.

During January, flower and seed catalogs were eagerly studied. The rare but occasional "June in January" day with temperatures in the 60s would be celebrated as a welcome preview of coming attractions. By February some residents dug up roots of sassafras trees, and boiled them to make sassafras tea which was considered a great "spring tonic". Anywhere that there was a swamp-like area it would be filled with small frogs which in spring-time made rather high pitched peeping noises which sounded somewhat like "knee deep". Most referred to them as "peep frogs". Usually they first would be heard in the evening after a relatively warm day in early March, signaling to us that spring was coming. However, if temperatures later dropped below freezing the frogs again would remain silent until the next "warm" day; that always seemed to happen. Many Galloway residents believed that spring really would not arrive until the frogs had been "frozen" twice after their initial peeping session. When they peeped again for the third time, often in mid-April, it was cause for celebration, and time to start looking to see if any crocus were growing up out of the snow, any daffodil buds had formed or, better yet, had anyone spotted a robin. If the latter happened it was to be reported so that an announcement could be printed in the Franklin newspaper. We knew then that the juneberry trees soon would be blooming, some seeds finally could be planted, and by early May leaves would be bursting out, apple orchards would be in full bloom, birds would be nesting, and it soon would be time to mow the lawn.

Summer would follow with generally pleasant weather. No homes on Galloway of which I was aware had air conditioning. On the occasional very hot night in July we might push a bed close to a screened open window and await cool breezes which usually came by midnight. Then would come September with its occasional frost, or even light snow, prompting comments such as, "Old man winter is just around the corner". But, we could still look forward to early October when the countryside would be covered with brilliant leaves, and November and December when "huntin" season, Thanksgiving, and family Christmas holidays would arrive. After that it was time to make sure there were ample supplies of coal or wood for heating, and that orders for spring seed and flower catalogs were being readied!

Galloway Life During World War II. One dictionary definition of an adventure is "an unusual or stirring experience". In a sense the many life changes brought about by WW II fit that description, both individually and collectively. Unusual experiences occurred over much of the world, and Galloway was no exception. Although our tiny piece of the world was spared the tragedy experienced so many places, the life changes we experienced can be classified as adventures. Certainly this was true from the perspective of a pre- adolescent child such as myself.

We all had heard of Hitler and Nazi Germany via News of the Day programs at movie theaters, and probably had learned at least of the existence of a country called Japan in our elementary school classes. But as children it is unlikely that war was on any of our minds. I have been told that on December 7th, 1941 I was playing with some toys behind Colonia when my sister Judy came to tell me, "The Japs have bombed Pearl Harbor". I responded, "So what?", and went back to playing. Within a few days all of us began to realize "what".

Because the nearby oil fields and refineries were essential to the war effort, there was fear that the area could become a target for bombers or sabotage. We had regular air raid drills at Galloway and in the schools. At night when an alarm would sound (probably the Rocky Grove Fire Dept. whistle) all lights had to be extinguished, and Mr. Ernest Frankenberger, our local air raid warden, would survey the neighborhood. Any house displaying even the tiniest light, such as from a cigarette, could be fined. At school an air raid drill was announced by the class-change buzzer emitting the Morse code sound sequence for the letter "V", as in "V for victory". We then were quickly herded to a mid-building hall where a teacher would lead us in singing songs such as "Remember Pearl Harbor" and "Praise the Lord and Pass the Ammunition" until the drill was over.

Our parents were urged to buy war bonds which, as I recall, might cost $37.50, but later be worth $50.00. And as children we were urged to gradually fill a small book with special 10 cent war stamps until it was worth the price of a bond. We also were asked to save tinfoil as from chewing gum wrappers, roll it into an increasingly larger ball and bring it to school to aid the war effort. Since metals were in great demand many communities would donate Civil War cannons from their parks to be melted down.

Soon rationing began of food, tires, fuels and other materials needed for the war. I especially recall limits on meats, sugar, tires and gasoline. After a few months into the war, if one's car tires or inner tubes wore out and could not be retreaded or patched there were no new ones to be had. An occasional person, in desperation, would take all tires off the rims and try to travel without tires. I recall that once in a while we would hear a car very noisily "riding on the rims" down Highway 417. Perhaps rim steel was tougher in those days. Once during the height of the war several of us children from Galloway had coaxed my dad to take us in his 1937 Ford to Oil City's Hasson Park which had a pool and large playground. On the way home at the junction of the Oil City-Franklin Road and Front Street of Rocky Grove a tire went flat. With no spare, we all had to walk home. I believe a neighbor later retrieved the tire, and the tube was patched so that our family again had wheels. All car owners were assigned gasoline stamps bearing the letter A, B or C which designated the amount of gasoline they were allowed to purchase within a given period of time. Persons with jobs deemed essential for the war effort were allowed more than others. The result was a major restriction of travel, such that for most Galloway residents the eighteen mile round trip to Oil City was a rare treat.

But, of course, our sacrifices on the home front were minor compared to those of most of the men on the war fronts. "Able-bodied" men under forty and with no children were drafted into military service upon turning eighteen. Many others volunteered, including some women who joined to become WACS, WAVES or WAFS. Although I don' t recall names of any persons in the military from Galloway, I imagine there were some who "went to war". Several men from my sister Margie's RGHS class of 1942 served, with at least one, Harry Hummel I believe, being killed in action. Adults often spoke in hushed tones of the growing numbers of "gold star" families in the county.

Although we had access to radio news of war developments, for some reason it seemed to me that our grocery delivery boy was a source of latest news. Perhaps he had a friend with a short wave radio and could receive news of local men, or of developments not shared with the general public; or maybe he just made up "fake news". Over the years I often have wondered about his sources. Specific bits of news which I sensed as a boy were of especially great importance to my parents concerned major advances of the Red (Russian) Army against the forces of Germany, the heroics of the English RAF pilots as they saved England from German invasion until U. S. and other allied forces could come to the country's aid, the D-day invasion, the end of the war against Germany (VE Day), the Doolittle "thirty second" air raid on Tokyo early in the war, and, of course, development of the atomic bomb.

Many local men, including my father, went daily by special bus for some time to work at a munitions plant at Geneva, PA. And, while I don't remember any local "Rosie the riveters", I know that several women from Galloway filled positions formerly held by men at the CPT.

And then one warm and memorable afternoon in mid-August, of 1945 several Galloway boys, and a few girls, had gone to the old ball field behind the church. There we were to meet some of similar age from nearby Oak Hill for a baseball game. I recall that several of the slightly older boys were teasing me, saying they knew a thirteen year old girl from Oak Hill was coming, and they were going to arrange for me, then age twelve, to get my "first kiss" from her. That team had not yet arrived, and I remember that during our batting practice I had just proudly caught, bare-handed, a line drive between second and third base when we heard the RGVFD alarm sounding non-stop. And since the weather was right for sound to travel up from Rocky Grove that day, we also heard church bells ringing. Some wondered aloud what could be going on, and then one said, "Maybe the war is over". At that point baseball equipment was thrown aside, and we all took off running for our homes. We never found out whether our informal Galloway team or the Oak Hill group was the better team; and several years passed before my first kiss!

That August night my family, along with what seemed like half the population of the county, went down to Franklin where all of Liberty Street and the city park were so crowded with very noisy celebrating people that few cars could get through. And those which did were honking horns non-stop. There certainly was good cause for celebration, Just a couple of weeks earlier news reports were claiming that we must prepare for an eventual land invasion of Japan which was likely to result in several hundreds of thousands of casualties. I recall that in my twelve year old mind it seemed as if Superman had come down from Krypton in the form of the Enola Gay, the plane from which the atomic bomb was dropped on Hiroshima, bringing a quick end to the war.

A Big Buck Story. The title for this next "adventure" story could have been "The Siefer Buck", although as will be shown, that could be a misnomer. One afternoon in November of 1949 I was squirrel hunting with my Marlin 22, sitting beside the spring on the northeast slope of Groundhog Hill. I had seen no squirrels, but suddenly a buck deer emerged from the woods about fifty yards below me and headed straight for the spring. Upon sensing my presence he stopped about 20 yards away, looked at me for a while, then snorted and ran away. Now, this was no ordinary buck. He probably weighed in the vicinity of 175 pounds. And, rather than first emerging relatively straight up from his skull before spreading out as with most buck deer, his antlers turned outward at an angle on each side and continued nearly horizontally for maybe twelve inches before symmetrically curving upward for what I estimated to be about 16 to 18 inches. In addition to the main antler tines, he had three more tines on each side; that is, he was a large, wide-antlered, eight-point buck.

Being a seventeen-year-old hunter in search of his first deer, this buck seemed like it might possibly be it, and what a trophy it would be! So, a few weeks later at 7:00 AM on the first day of deer season, I was sitting in the same spot, Ithaca 37 at the ready, hoping that deer would return. As was common in the Pennsylvania woods between 7:00 and 8:00 AM on the first day of the season, many shots rang out for miles around, and echoed through the hills and valleys. But I was especially interested in one series of somewhere between eight and twelve quite evenly spaced shots coming from about a quarter mile away on a ridge in the vicinity of what is labeled Montana Drive on today's satellite maps. I assumed shots so evenly spaced must have been from one hunter's gun rather than from several hunters, and probably fired by a poor shot using one of the older lever action Winchester or Marlin rifles with magazines holding fourteen or fifteen cartridges. But, I also knew that so many shots indicated the deer may still be running, and therefore might be coming by my stand any minute. It did not; and the day passed without my seeing a single deer.

For several days I watched News Herald announcements concerning deer having been taken, but did not notice any evidence that the "big buck" was among them. In subsequent years I sometimes hunted deer in the same general area, including one evening on the same ridge where I had heard the string of shots. At the far eastern end of that ridge just before it slopes down toward Two-mile Run there was at the time a small stand of very large trees. Some were around five feet in diameter at the base and very tall. My uncle Wilbur Rogers once told me that this was the last virgin forest remaining in the county. All I know for certain is they were big, and that evening the wind was still, a soft, light snow was slowly falling and the woods seemed eerily silent. Suddenly a great horned owl with a very wide wing span flew from high up in one of the trees hooting very loudly as it headed down the ridge. Somewhat shaken by the sudden sound, and noting that it was nearly 4:30 I hurried on home. If I had been a believer in reincarnation, I might have thought the "big buck" actually had been shot, and had come back as the owl, perhaps saying to me, "Well, you have been looking for me here for years, so here I am. Hope I startled you as much as you did me back at the spring that day."

But the story doesn't end there. In 1970, twenty-one years after the deer sighting at the spring, Galloway's then-oldest resident, and once a friend of my grandmother, Ms. Emma Siefer, died at the age of 104. Her home furnishings were being sold, and my mother, first wife, and daughter Brenda went to the sale which was held in her house on the left hand side of Warren Road just beyond the Schiffer farm. If standing on the front porch of that house and looking toward the east, one could see the trees on the beginning of the ridge where I had heard the long string of shots in 1949. And, on a wall in the house there was a mounted eight-point deer head with wide spaced antlers which looked to me very much like the "big buck"! I didn't know his name, but I asked a man there if he knew the history of that deer mount. As best I can recall, he said it was taken near there by Mr. Siefer back in the 1940s, and he believed that he did hunt with an older lever action rifle. So, was it the buck? Lots of circumstantial evidence says "yes". In 2016 while at Dawndi's restaurant I was telling this story to a couple of men who lived nearby. One said, "Well, I saw a buck with wide-spread antlers just as you describe a few nights ago over in one of the Schiffer fields". He and I wondered if it possibly could be one of the Siefer buck's descendants. I didn't ask, but perhaps should have, whether he also had heard the call of a great horned owl. If he had, well.....!

Fire-fighting Tales. The Rocky Grove Volunteer Fire Department and Relief Association (RGVFD) was formed in 1933, so in a sense I grew up with it. A great many past and present Galloway residents have interacted with that Department over the past eighty plus years, whether using their fire-fighting services, serving as members, attending their annual fairs, or enjoying their firemen parades and marching bands.

My first interaction with it happened late in the morning of April 14, 1941, an "Easter Monday" school holiday. A brush and structure fire occurred which may have been the most expensive in terms of monetary loss of any Galloway fire. Excerpts from my older sister's diary of that day read: "What a day! About noon, a fire started on the lease just below our garage. Just before the flames reached the garage the wind shifted and saved it". "Over 100 people were here". "Three or four fire companies were here. Some excitement!". I recall being in the living room of Colonia and hearing my Uncle Jim Rogers, then a lease worker, loudly calling to my mother to call the RGVFD. I looked out a window and saw about an eight foot high wall of flames in the dead sumac and blackberry brush sixty yards away headed directly toward an oil well tank and our house. The latter was separated only by our oval shaped driveway. As my older sister evacuated my younger sister and me to a field above the house, my mother found that the RGVFD was fighting another fire elsewhere, the Franklin Department refused to respond to out-of-city fires, and the other nearby departments at Reno and Cooperstown also were out on calls. My eighty-one year old grandfather then arrived with a garden hose to wet-down the garage. However, by that time the wind direction suddenly had shifted from south to west, sparing the house and garage but engulfing storage tanks and pumping apparatus of two oil wells as well as a large pumphouse. It was spreading rapidly to the east where many more wells and another pumphouse were located. At that point, to the surprise of all, as we looked up toward Infield Drive we saw a car rushing back the road. I recall one man was standing on a running board of the car, just as in gangster movies of the day where "G-men" armed with sub-machine guns often stood while pursuing gangsters. We learned later that the car held five or six men from Dempseytown, "armed" not with guns but with Indian fire pumps each containing five gallons of water and carried like a knapsack on one's back. Using a hand operated pump mechanism they could send a stream of water thirty feet or so to quite effectively quench flames of a brush fire. I never knew how these men learned of the fire, but do know they stopped it within a few yards of the second pumphouse, and no more wells burned. Perhaps they were the nucleus of what eleven years later became the Oakland Township Volunteer Fire Department. Later that afternoon the RGVFD and others arrived to guard the fire from flaring up again.

My second encounter occurred two years later on a spring day when four or five of us pre-teenage boys decided to try to clear the old Galloway ball field of a winter's accumulation of high dead grass and small shrubs so that we would have a place for ball games. We had no power mowers or string trimmers in those days, and it was very slow going trying to clear it with sickles. Someone came up with the idea that we could safely burn it off if we burned just one small area at a time, being sure to use our shirts to "whack" the flames out each time before proceeding to the next small burn area. But, nature didn't cooperate. It wasn't long until a gust of wind widened an area so large we could not extinguish it, and the fire was expanding into the brush and heading toward oil wells. We quickly scattered. I never knew where the others went, but I ran the entire half mile or so to get my parents to call the RGVFD. No one was home, so I ran on up to the Frankenberger home where I collapsed on their lawn saying "fire" and pointing toward the west where smoke clouds could be seen rising above the trees behind the church. Very shortly the fire alarm sounded, and I recovered enough to walk back to greet the firemen when they arrived in the RGVFD's "emergency car". That was a pre-war panel truck converted to a fire truck, and capable of carrying a few men and Indian fire pumps. The truck could not go the entire way to the site of the fire because of a low rod line across the road, so it was necessary for them to shoulder the pumps and walk the last 100 yards or more. It was war time, and most of the firemen were middle aged or older. I recall one saying, "I'm too old for this!" Nevertheless, they made it to the fire and extinguished it before any wells were burned. Both my father and the owner of the oil lease arrived as the firemen were leaving. I remember the owner saying, "That RGVFD is worth its weight in gold". He then angrily suggested that I deserved "a good licken", but mellowed a little when dad reminded him that it was I who had run for help. From that time on I was a fan of the Department, having as my "heroes" people such as Lee Shingledecker and Ralph Brannon, both of whom served as fire chief during some of the early years.

During middle years of the 1940s while sitting in RGHS classes I would hear the fire alarm sound, and watch to see if the open-cab 1929 LaFrance truck of the RGVFD would be going north past the school. The station was sixty yards or so downhill from the school at the corner of Phipps Street, so they would be going uphill, and no more than about twenty miles per hour. However, it was exciting to watch them, and daydream about the day I would become a fireman. I believe I was nineteen when that day came. For the next nine years, with two years out for Army duty, I was an avid fireman. I rode the trucks to many fires along with men such as George "Snuffy" Smith who was chief for many of those years, Mel Campbell, Bob Parker, Dick Hefferman, Fritz Rial, and Tom Shuffstall. The latter is considered by many to have been the best known and most influential of all persons in the history of the RGVFD. It was a time of great camaraderie and excitement, not only fighting fires, but also participating in the many fireman parades and the annual fair. During the summer we often took a truck and the Department's marching band to towns as far away as Jamestown, N. Y. and suburbs of Pittsburgh to participate in their parades. They would return the favor by participating in ours. Riding on the platform at the back of the truck and waving to pretty girls in the crowds lining the streets was great fun. There were marching bands in most parades, and ours often won an award as best. Many local people will recall those parades in Rocky Grove and nearby towns, and the music of our marching band led many years by pretty drum majorette Betty Snyder (later Betty Adams after her marriage to Jack Adams, the RGHS athlete mentioned earlier).

A great many Galloway residents attended the annual fair held in mid- to-late summer to ride the "whip", "octopus", Ferris wheel or merry- go round, or try to win a prize throwing a ball or shooting special cartridges from a Winchester pump action rifle. Many participated in bingo games or ate at the Ladies Auxiliary cook tent where much of the food was donated by women from the surrounding region.

In the following paragraphs I describe a few "firemen stories" which may be of special interest to readers whose parents or grandparents, or they themselves, were involved with the RGVFD during this period. And, a few present firemen also may find it interesting to read these bits of RGVFD history.

Most of the fire calls to which we responded were forest fires, perhaps more appropriately labeled brush fires. They were fought primarily with Indian fire pumps and rakes unless we could get close enough to use a hose with water from tanks on the trucks. Many of the structure fires of those days involved barns containing hay which often were burned to the ground by the time we arrived. April was by far our busiest time of the year, especially on weekends. Each Saturday morning in April I would be up early, stop at a local store (usually Mrs. Doubt's store) for a quart of milk and candy bars for lunch, and go to the fire station to await our first call. By the mid-to-late 1950s we had a pickup truck, but our basic brush fire truck was a white, partially home-made truck of the "squared type" somewhat resembling many of the ambulances of later years. Firemen could sit on benches inside where the 600 gallon water tank also was located, or, if desired, stand on a platform where a back bumper ordinarily would be. Although some of us preferred riding on the back, in retrospect that may have been the most dangerous part of our work. But, there were other potential dangers as indicated in the following paragraph.

One brush fire is especially memorable for me. On a late March afternoon we had been called to a site not far from the present Galloway church where a couple of acres of grass and brush were burning around where a house once had been. We knew to be careful because most old home sites had water wells which may not have completely filled in, and boards covering them may have rotted. With a full Indian tank on my back I was rushing toward the flames and did not notice what would have been a tell-tale change in the surface of the ground: a somewhat "softer" and different colored appearance. When I stepped on it I quickly sank in above my knees and seemed to be very slowly sinking further. Unable to move with the heavy load on my back, I was wondering if I was in quick-sand. For a few seconds I more or less "froze", both physically and mentally. Then I felt a tug under my arms and realized I was being lifted out, all 155 pounds of me, plus the fifty or so pounds of the Indian tank, by the strong arms of six foot two, 200 pound fellow fireman Dick Hefferman. It turned out I had fallen into a long abandoned cesspool, luckily no longer filled with its former content, but with soft dirt, leaves and other matter softened by rains and melting snow. For a long time I was teased about that "Jim and the cesspool" event.

I am not certain about the accuracy of some details of the next narrative. However, as I remember this event, and the story which circulated later among some firemen, it happened as follows. On a hot summer afternoon in the early to middle 1950s the Department received a phone call that, "all of downtown Stoneboro is burning and we need all the help we can get". We immediately headed out for that town roughly fifteen miles away. At that time we had no radios in our trucks, and, of course, cell phones had not been invented. Thus we had no way of knowing what was going on as we progressed toward the town. When we were within a mile or so we expected to see huge clouds of smoke on the horizon, but instead saw three or four other fire trucks going away from Stoneboro. Confused, we proceeded to the center of the town where we saw several more trucks parked, and heard yet another arriving. By then we knew it either was a false alarm, or some other town with a similar sounding name was ablaze. Tom Shuffstall was among the firemen who had arrived. He also was a justice of the peace, apparently with arrest powers. I was not a witness to what supposedly happened next, so cannot guarantee its truth. But a story circulated later that, on a hunch, Tom went into a bar in the middle of town, sat down beside a somewhat intoxicated man he judged to be what today might be referred to as a "person of interest", and struck up a conversation. Soon the man began laughing and telling how he had managed to "bring some life to this sleepy town by calling every fire department I could". At that point Tom supposedly placed him under arrest.

After graduating from Clarion College in 1956 I served in the Army for two years, and then taught school in Cleveland for the next two years. Thus, it was not until January of 1961 that I once again lived in the area, and spent much time with the RGVFD. By that time there had been many changes in the Department. For example, there were two pumper trucks in addition to the old LaFrance, and all departments in the county were equipped with radios which enabled communication between stations and trucks. Fire calls could be made to a central call center in Franklin, and any or all department alarms could be activated from there. Although Tom Shuffstall remained hghly influential, different persons such as Chuck Haun and Fred Hutchison were, or soon would be, elected chief or assistant chief.

The final story here concerns the last fire I fought with the Department. It also happens to be what for many years was, and perhaps still is, the second largest and most disastrous fire in the history of Franklin. On the evening of June 2, 1961 I was living at 119 ½ First Avenue in the Bleakley Hill section of Rocky Grove. The house was on a bluff overlooking parts of the city of Franklin. While mowing the front lawn I noticed an increasingly larger plume of dark smoke rising. Probably due to the noise of the mower, I had not heard the explosion which had occurred. This looked like smoke from an uncontrolled fire, so I shut off the mower. Two or three minutes later I heard the Franklin fire alarm (a large bell in those days), and assumed it was connected to the smoke I was seeing. Very quickly the smoke plume grew much larger, and, deciding it was likely that the Franklin Department soon would be calling us for assistance, I headed for the fire hall. Our alarm was sounding as I approached the hall. I parked and ran to jump on the back of a pumper which was just pulling out.

As we rounded Coefield's Corner we came upon a chaotic, and rather terrifying scene. Flames were shooting high above much of the city block- size Joy plant #3, smoke seemed to be everywhere, and small explosions were occurring. We were directed to a hydrant on the right side of 13th Street near the Erie railroad tracks, and ordered to connect a 2 ½ inch hose and direct water on and around the small Wolf's Head gasoline station beside the plant. Its underground tanks recently had been filled, and it was feared that if the flames reached it there might be a major explosion. We quickly did so, but after turning on the hydrant as we had been used to doing, no water flowed. For the next several minutes we stood there frustrated and wondering what to do next. Then a Franklin fireman appeared and explained that hydrant had two valves, both of which needed to be open. He proceeded to open the second one, and we finally were able to do as ordered. The station did not burn, nor did the tanks explode.

Meanwhile chaos continued at the scene. Our radio transmissions were filled with directions to the ten or eleven other county departments responding to requests for help in fighting the fire, or to "stand-by" at the Franklin station in case additional fires occurred. At the time few departments had trucks capable of pumping 1000 gallons or more per minute, but an exception was the department from the tiny village of Utica about fifteen miles away. Their truck was considered badly needed, not only because of its pumping capacity, but because it would be coming in from the north side of 13th Street, and not from south side which was clogged with Franklin fire equipment and other traffic. Ordinarily a radio transmission would be preceded by an identifying phrase such as "KGD 514 calling KGD xxx", but one I especially recall at the height of the fire dispensed with that as a panicked-sounding voice screamed, "Utica! Utica! where the hell are you?" The immediate response was, "We're coming in 322 wide open; this truck won't do over 60" (or maybe he said "70"; I'm not certain). I have always thought that transmission sort of summed up the situation at that point in. time.

After more than two hours of battling the fire the Joy plant was totally destroyed, but other structures behind the plant, and the offices and stores across 13th Street were saved by fire crews drenching the exteriors and roofs with water.

Even so, many windows there were broken, and there were reports of scorched curtains in some of the rooms facing the street. A column in the June 3rd edition of the News Herald reported that over a thousand spectators safely observed the fire from banks on the south side of French Creek. But others failed to heed police orders and tried to cross the bridge to get closer to the fire scene, sometimes blocking access by responding fire equipment.

Oil City radio station WKRZ maintained continuous reporting of the fire, including possibility of a major gasoline tank explosion. The latter caused great anxiety for my wife who was listening, and the next day she expressed her opinion that, as the father of a four month old child (our daughter Brenda), I should not be engaging in such life-threatening activities. I thought it over, and decided she probably was right. Anyway, brush fire season essentially was over by then, and in a few weeks we would be moving to Kent, Ohio where I would resume classes at Kent State. After that, school work, and some family illness consumed much of my time, a second child, Kent, was born, and we made several moves. There would have been very little time for further firefighting, and I never again rode with the RGVFD.

In 1986 while in Franklin for an RGHS class reunion I saw former chief "Snuffy" Smith sitting on the porch of his Parker Avenue home and stopped to visit. He remembered me, and we spent an hour or two reminiscing about the fifties good times. Then in 2016 at another RGHS reunion I stopped by the fire hall located since 1969 further north just off Rocky Grove Avenue. It is on a street re-named Shuffstall Avenue in honor of Tom Shuffstall who had passed on. I was amazed at the size and quality of equipment the RGVFD now possesses which we could not have dreamed of back then. When I told my guide that we used to wish for a 1000 gallon per minute pumper, and a 1000 gallon tanker truck, he pointed to what I believe he said was a 3000 gallon per minute pumper, and a 3000 gallon tanker. Then he pointed out at least one fully pump-and tank-equipped four-wheel drive pick-up truck for fighting brush fires. It appeared capable of clearing the top of Galloway Hill at 60 miles an hour.

Even today I still sense a rush of adrenaline when I hear fire truck sirens. And, sometimes I try to imagine today's RGHS boys, and possibly some girls, watching the big RGVFD trucks moving down the Avenue at forty-five or fifty miles per hour with sirens screaming and horns blaring, and wonder if they, too, daydream of the day they become firemen (or women). I bet they do.

As readers complete this chapter on 1937 -1965 society and culture of Galloway, some likely will believe the author must have been wearing rose-colored glasses while living there, or suspect he succumbed to the often-reported human tendency as one ages to remember the good and forget the bad. Perhaps they recall "revelations" about small-town America's corrupt, sinful or hypocritical behaviors presented in the late 1950s movie Peyton Place or the popular country song Harper Valley PTA of the late 1960s, and believe that Galloway could not have been immune to such. I would reply that I do remember instances indicative of lack of total immunity, and do realize that some things were "swept under the rug". Furthermore, it is true that there were aspects of life then which today a great many, if not all, persons would consider unacceptable. Women had restricted career choices (which will it be, teacher, nurse, secretary, or housewife?), medical and dental care often left something to be desired, PETA would frown on some of our behaviors toward animals, corporal punishment often was harmful, and winters were harsh. And, in my role as a psychologist at the local mental health center during the mid-1960s I was surprised at times to learn of certain happenings in families from the county. Those usually were alcohol and/or sex-related, but always harmful to mental health and sometimes illegal. Nevertheless, I still maintain that the vast majority of Galloway residents of that era were honest, friendly, trusting, trustworthy, intelligent, God-fearing, and hard-working persons, commensurate with the descriptions and stories presented above. All in all, a good place to have lived.

I have no reason to believe that the above description of Galloway residents has changed greatly, for better or worse. But, fifty-five years have passed since 1965, and even back then, to paraphrase a Bob Dylan song, "the times they were a-changing". Although change may not have been as rapid at Galloway as in many cities, it almost certainly occurred there as well. Hopefully, resourceful residents adapted accordingly, and have retained their positive personal characteristics. Certainly many should have anticipated change, since, after all, those of us who spent afternoons and evenings at the Orpheum Theater knew that Time Marches On.....so it does.

Chapter 6

Postscript

After leaving for graduate school in Nashville in the Fall of 1965 I had sporadic contact with Galloway. My mother continued to live in the old Rogers-Evans home until illness forced a move to our home in Columbia, S.C. where she passed away in July of 1979 at the age of eighty-four. During the preceding dozen or so years my first wife Margaret and I, and our children, Brenda and Kent, always spent Christmas, and three or four weeks each summer at Galloway in the old home. Many of the neighbors I had known earlier had moved or died, the oil leases no longer were active, and most of the lease roads eventually became overgrown to the point they were impassable to anything other than dirt bikes, ATVs, horses or foot traffic. However, Brenda has many fond memories of those years, spending much quality time with her Grandma Evans, as well as with her grandparents on her mother's (Bashline) side of the family in Knox. And my son remembers well the many days he enjoyed riding his dirt bikes over the thousands of unrestricted acres of former oil leases,. During that time he graduated from a Honda 50, to a Hodaka, to a Yamaha, to man-sized Hondas. He still has pictures in his ATV repair shop of the old Galloway "dirt bike gang" members such as Bobby Ross, Kelly Young, Craig Westover, and himself.

Brenda Evans with her grandmother Evans and aunt Judy (1972) & Kent Evans, age 9, on right with early Galloway "dirt bike gang" members (1973)

Several times during the 1980s and 90s, and as late as 2006, Kent and I visited the area largely for the purpose of his having a chance to again ride the Galloway trails.

One especially memorable visit took place during the summer of 1997. My sister, Judy, persuaded the family renting the old Rogers-Evans home to leave for a few days and visit relatives so that my two sisters, my son Kent and I could have the house to ourselves. A true sentimental journey. We slept in bedrooms we had occupied in years gone by, and had buckwheat cake and sausage breakfasts in the kitchen. One day I elected to take my Browning BL22 rifle and walk some of the trails I had hiked years ago. However, I worried about how the sight of a man carrying a gun would be received by present residents. My first encounter was with Ernest Montgomery when I crossed his land on my way to the site of the old Galloway ball field. He recognized me immediately, and assured me that I was always welcome on his property. There was no mention of the rifle. Later I walked over Infield Drive to explore some side roads which branched off from it. Shortly I was hailed by Red Ross who at that time lived in a mobile home along the road. After some friendly conversation about our recent lives, I confided that I was concerned that residents might be upset by my carrying a gun. He looked rather puzzled, then said, "Why would they be"? That evening, leaving the rifle in my truck. I visited what had been, and I believe still was, the Voyager Inn on Liberty Street in Franklin. While seated at the bar and enjoying a Rolling Rock beer and sandwich I watched couples on the small dance floor slow dancing to country music. I overheard two young women alternately discussing favorite Tri-city Speedway memories, and their plans for a fall bear hunt. As I left and walked toward my truck, a car radio was playing the Conway Twitty song, Tight Fittin' Jeans. By the end of that day I knew I was "back home"!

By 2006 much land had been purchased by individuals, several new homes had been built, a large golf course covered several acres, much of the land had been leased by lumber companies, and horseback trail-riding seemed to have become more popular than dirt-bike riding. Along with this came some threatening "No Trespassing" and "No Dirt Bikes or ATVs" signs, and verbal reminders from some that riding horses and dirt bikes on the same trails did not mix well.

After 2006, my wife, Martha, and I returned to the Galloway area several times in conjunction with RGHS reunions. On August 8th following the 2016 reunion I drove up to the beautiful log home of Mark Jacoby, his Mother Ardythe (Keith) Jacoby, and step-daughter Megan. It is located a few yards below the crest of the southernmost of the "twin peaks" referred to earlier. It is on the upper portion of acres which for many years were sites of the Willis Frankenberger and Charles Snyder residences. Although Mark was not home, I was able to spend a long, enjoyable afternoon sharing Galloway memories with Ardythe who at that time was 90 years of age.

The next day my wife and I enjoyed a very special memory-sharing dinner meeting at Dawndi's Restaurant with surviving members of older Galloway families. Others in attendance included Betty (Free) Morrison, Judy (Jacoby) Lusher, Grace (Jacoby) Solle, Marlyn (Orr) Sutley and husband Bob, Peggy (Cheers) McClelland, Ardythe (Keith) Jacoby, and Virgil Keith. The latter three have since passed away.

In the Fall of 2017 I returned to Galloway with my daughter for funeral services for my sister Judy. We buried her ashes at the nearby Bethel Cemetery which is the location of graves of my parents, maternal grandparents and great grandparents. Only a few almost unrecognizable remnants of Colonia existed, and the old Rogers-Evans home as well as most, if not all, of the "lease houses" were gone. Only a few home movies and pictures, and lots of memories remain of the Galloway of old.

However, the area still has positive features today. For example, Lucky Hills Golf Course and the associated Dawndi's Restaurant with its great food, friendly service and beautiful view of the Patchel Run valley now are Galloway jewels. And, for hunters I understand that, although the grouse may be all but gone, deer hunting remains great, and bears and wild turkeys now are plentiful. Fishermen now can enjoy excellent fishing for bass, trout and muskellunge in the 104 acre Justus Lake at nearby Two Mile Run County Park. And, perhaps there still are 6 to16 inch brook trout in Patchel Run!

According to recent satellite pictures of the Galloway area some new roads or lanes exist, suggesting that the population may be growing; that is, unless roads such as those labeled Schiff Lane, Wingate Drive, and Montana Drive simply are old, uninhabited lease roads assigned names by the map makers. Related to the topic of population growth, on my last visit I speculated with a Galloway resident about the village's future. I suggested that, since the area now has city water, plenty of flat land with attractive building sites, and access to excellent schools it may become a magnet for new businesses and/or residential development. He looked upset, and responded, "I hope to hell not!" Obviously, "Galloway as is", and "Galloway as was" have special meaning for many who now reside there, as well as for those of us who once lived there "back in the day".

References

Babcock, C.A. (1919). Venango County, Pennsylvania: Her Pioneers and People, Volume 1. Chicago: J. H. Beers & Company.

Eaton, S. J. M. (1866). Petroleum: A History of the Oil Region of Venango County, Pennsylvania. Philadelphia: J.P. Skelly & Company.

Kay, J. L. and Smith, C. M. (1976). Pennsylvania Postal History. Lawrence Massachusetts: Quarteman Publications, Inc.

Printed in the United States
By Bookmasters